CW00957612

OPENING DOORS: HELPING PEOPLE ON LOW INCOME SECURE PRIVATE RENTED ACCOMMODATION

Julie Rugg

RESEARCH REPORT

CENTRE FOR HOUSING POLICY
University of York

Published by:
Centre for Housing Policy
University of York
York YO1 5DD
Telephone 01904 433691
Fax 01904 432318

ISBN 1 874797 75 7

Typeset by Joanne Gatenby in the Centre for Housing Policy
Printed by York Publishing Services Ltd

The **Joseph Rowntree Foundation** has supported this project as part of its programme of research and innovative development projects, which it hopes will be of value to policy makers and practitioners. The facts presented and views expressed in this report however, are those of the author and not necessarily those of the Foundation.

Acknowledgements

(handwritten annotation): "Chloe" -> 0121 - 486 2808 Legny Jamp " " 071 - 2194190

This report, and the research on which it is based, could not have been completed without the help of a great number of people. Thanks are due to the Joseph Rowntree Foundation which funded the research, and to Theresa McDonagh, Principal Research Manager, for her guidance. The research was fortunate in its Advisory Group, members of which were always available to offer helpful comment and advice. The Advisory Group included: Sally Burns, Senior Environmental Health Officer, Doncaster Metropolitan Council; Niall Cooper, Churches National Housing Coalition; John Critchfield, Department of Social Security; Louise Dominian, Department of the Environment; Hugh Driskell, Community Service Manager, Nottingham City Council; Simon Goss, Cardiff Bond Board; Ronnie Hill, York Detached Youth Work Project; Mike Jenn, Quaker Social Action; Fraser Neasham, Shelter; Liz Phelps, National Association of Citizens Advice Bureaux; Simon Prendergast, Oxford Citizens Housing Association Ltd; and Geoff Randall, Research and Information Services.

Thanks are expressed to all the access scheme managers who took the time to complete our survey form. Particular gratitude is due to the managers of the case study schemes, who took sometimes quite considerable time to explain the working of their schemes, and who helped to set up interviews with clients and landlords. Thanks are also expressed to the clients and landlords who were willing to be interviewed.

Finally, thanks are given to staff members of the Centre for Housing Policy: Lora Sanderling for her help in completing the fieldwork; Joanne Gatenby for her help in the task of report preparation; and David Rhodes, who read preliminary drafts. Thanks are also given to Peter Kemp, now at the Centre for Housing Research and Urban Studies in Glasgow, for his supervision of the early stages of the research.

The author

Julie Rugg is a research fellow in the Centre for Housing Policy at the University of York.

Contents

Chapter Four:
Dealing with Landlords   **31**

Section Two : Services Schemes Offered

Chapter Five:
Help Finding Somewhere to Live   **41**

Chapter Six:
Help with Deposits   **53**

Chapter Seven:
Help with Housing Benefit and Rent in Advance   **63**

List of tables

List of appendix tables

Executive Summary

Introduction

▶ This report comprises an evaluation of help given to people on low incomes who are trying to secure access to accommodation in the private rented sector. Three broad types of scheme were examined. Deposit schemes gave help with the requirement to pay a bond, sometimes through offering cash loans and sometimes through issuing a bond which guaranteed reimbursement to the landlord in the case of damage or theft, for example. Rent in advance schemes helped by giving a loan to cover rent in advance payments. Accommodation registers assisted people by helping them to find somewhere to live.

▶ Although a consensus has arisen that the growth of deposit schemes, rent in advance schemes and accommodation registers (all together in this report termed 'access schemes') is a valuable development, there is a wide variation in the way in which these services are delivered.

▶ This report is based on research which aimed to gain a clearer impression of the nature of the access schemes currently operating, and to complete an evaluation of different approaches to the delivery of access help. The research used both quantitative and qualitative methods, and comprised a postal survey of 161 schemes, 11 interviews with scheme managers, 39 interviews with scheme clients and 43 interviews with landlords involved with schemes.

Chapter one: the issue of access

▶ A number of obstacles face people on low incomes who want to secure accommodation in the private rented sector. These include fears about the inability to afford any possible shortfall between the rent charged and the housing benefit payable; meeting the requirement to pay deposits and/or rent in advance; the unwillingness of landlords to let to people on housing benefit; and the poor quality of accommodation at the bottom end of the market all of which mean that choice is further limited. Having to deal with all these obstacles together means that the search for somewhere to stay can often be protracted.

▸   The policy response to access problems has been the encouragement of two sorts of initiative: accommodation registers, the development of which has been boosted by the availability of s73 funding; and deposit guarantee and rent in advance schemes, the establishment of which by local authorities has received a general consent.

Chapter two: access schemes - development, status and funding

▸   Most of the schemes were established in the 1990s. The accommodation register schemes had been running slightly longer than the deposit guarantee schemes.

▸   Fifty-six per cent of schemes were being run by voluntary sector organisations; 30 per cent by local authorities; and 9 per cent by housing associations. A small proportion of schemes - five per cent - were managed jointly by two or more sorts of agency.

▸   Most of the schemes extended and complemented work already being done to help a group of people in housing need - for example, by local authority homeless units, or by voluntary sector projects offering move-on help to people in hostels. Only a small number of the schemes were 'stand alone', having no parent organisation, and were perhaps more dependent on forging links with other agencies to refer clients and deal with any necessary client support.

▸   Statistics relating to the funding of local authority schemes were not available. However, other material indicated that the majority of local authority schemes were funded through the general budget of their housing department, and there was a high degree of confidence that this funding would be available over the long term: 77 per cent of local authority schemes considered that securing long-term funding was not a problem at all.

▸   More information was available on the funding of voluntary sector schemes: the majority had an annual income of £30,000 or less. A fifth of the schemes were wholly reliant on s73 funding, with a further fifth receiving the majority of their funding from this source. Reliance on charitable giving was extensive. The overriding characteristic of voluntary sector funding was its precarious nature.

Eighty-three per cent of voluntary sector schemes considered securing long-term funding to be constantly or frequently a problem.

▶ Seventy-three schemes gave guarantees to cover bonds. Sixty-three per cent of these schemes had bond funds of £10,000 or less: the average total was £11,163. Local authority guarantee schemes were more likely to have financed their guarantee fund internally. Voluntary sector schemes were more reliant on churches, charitable trusts and private donations. Amongst the voluntary sector case study guarantee schemes, there was little evidence of any long-term planning to secure top-up financing to the guarantee fund to compensate for sums paid out to landlords.

Chapter three: dealing with clients

▶ The average number of clients helped by all schemes in 1993/4 was 92. However, there was considerable diversity between schemes according to their status and type. Local authority schemes and voluntary sector schemes helped, on average, 60 and 104 clients respectively. Schemes giving cash help with deposits and schemes not giving such help assisted, on average, 74 and 117 clients respectively.

▶ Almost all the case study scheme managers said that they were able to meet all the demand for their services, although there were some constraints on throughputs, since the limited supply of accommodation sometimes created bottlenecks of clients who had been assessed, but for whom no accommodation was available.

▶ The majority of schemes (86 per cent) operated one or more restrictions on the type of client they intended to help. Voluntary sector schemes were more likely to have restrictions which included only taking people who were non-statutory homeless, only taking young people and only taking single people. Local authority schemes, by contrast, were more likely to have restrictions which included only taking statutory homeless people, only taking families, and only taking people who were on the council's housing waiting list.

▶ There were some restrictions which were more generally applied, and these included only taking on people who were capable of living independently. Scheme managers commented that this restriction was applied for a range of reasons: clients with more intense support needs should be helped by the social services;

this sort of client should not be in private rented housing; and if taken on by a scheme, clients with support needs would endanger a scheme's relations with landlords, who tended not to want this sort of person as a tenant.

▶ Most schemes took on their clients through a range of routes. On average, 37 per cent of clients were taken on through self-referral, 25 per cent were referred from other parts of the parent organisation, 15 per cent were referred from local voluntary organisations, and 24 per cent were referred from statutory organisations. Local authorities were more likely to take on a higher proportion of their clients through internal referrals from other parts of the housing department.

▶ Looking at the way in which referrals worked in practice, through the examples of the case study schemes, it was common for the process to be open and informal, although in one case a more formal contractual system of referral had been set up. Schemes were generally happy with the system of referrals which had been set up, since the clients who had been sent were usually appropriate. Some schemes complained that social services departments had, on occasion, sent clients who did not have well-established care packages.

Chapter four: dealing with landlords

▶ Most of the schemes collated information on the rental market in their area, usually through keeping a list of landlords and their properties. The information contributed to schemes' understanding of the particular rental market in which they were operating, and informed decisions on which services to offer.

▶ There was a contrast between local authority schemes and voluntary sector schemes in terms of their experience of limitations in the supply of accommodation. Only one third of local authorities considered the limited supply of accommodation to be constantly or frequently a problem, compared with 85 per cent of voluntary sector schemes which reported accommodation supply to be always or frequently a problem. The dissimilar experiences suggest that actual supply of accommodation was in some areas less a problem than schemes' ability to gain access to it.

▶ It was inadvisable to generalise about schemes' relationships with landlords, since different experiences were evident according to the type of landlord and in some cases also according to the status of the scheme. For example, both types of scheme could secure a good supply of accommodation at the bottom end of the rented market; and local authority schemes were more likely to be able to secure the co-operation of 'reluctant' or inexperienced landlords who wanted the security of dealing with 'the Council'.

▶   Voluntary sector schemes which wanted to deal with landlords further up the rental market were compelled to offer a greater degree of financial security, such as payments of rent until the housing benefit was processed, and deposit guarantees.

▶   Almost all the schemes imposed some restrictions on the landlords they dealt with, which included not having convictions for harassment or illegal eviction, and charging a reasonable rents which would be unlikely to incur a shortfall. Schemes also often tried only to deal with landlords having good management practices such as offering good quality accommodation which meets health and safety requirements.

▶   The imposition of restrictions on landlords also highlighted distinctions between scheme status and scheme type. Local authority schemes and schemes offering financial help with deposits were both more likely to be able to impose a wider range of restrictions on the landlords they dealt with.

▶   In practice, schemes were sometimes unable to impose restrictions on the landlords they dealt with if the client was willing to enter into the tenancy despite the advice given by the scheme. It was commonly the case that clients, in desperate need of somewhere to stay, were willing to go into properties below the standard normally approved by the scheme.

▶   Thirty-six per cent of schemes kept a list of bad landlords, with whom they would not deal, and 46 per cent kept a list of good landlords. Good landlords were judged to be those who responded quickly to requests for repairs, gave notice before they visited the property, and stuck to the terms of the tenancy agreement.

▶   On average, 47 per cent of clients were placed in self-contained flats or houses. Again, however, there were distinctions according to the status and type of the scheme. Local authority schemes were more likely than voluntary sector schemes to place a higher proportion of their clients in self-contained accommodation. Similarly, schemes giving cash help with deposits were also less likely to be reliant on the use of HMOs than schemes not giving such help.

Chapter five: help finding somewhere to live

▶   Most of the schemes (89 per cent) helped people to find somewhere to live by giving them access to vacancies and matching them up with suitable accommodation. Schemes also helped in the setting up of tenancies.

▶   It was possible for schemes to use one or more of three different types of accommodation register during this process: registers of landlords who met established criteria (approved landlord registers); lists of vacancies from approved landlords (approved vacancy lists) and lists of vacancies not checked by the scheme (unvetted vacancy lists).

▶   Schemes were often unable to describe their rationale for the way in which they ordered their information on landlords and vacancies. The lack of a planned approach may be explained by the fact that the registers had developed in an *ad hoc* way over time, and were often informally kept, since the number of landlords a scheme might deal with could be small.

▶   Schemes helped people find somewhere to live by giving them information on vacancies. Two approaches were taken: collating vacancy lists, which were then given to the client; or supporting the client in the search process by looking through newspapers with them, and taking them to see properties. Offering vacancy lists gave the client the opportunity to exercise choice and initiative, but entailed spending time keeping the list up to date. Supporting the search process was also time consuming, but the time was spent with the client and so offered the chance for the scheme to gain a greater understanding of the client's housing needs.

▶   Most schemes made some assessment of whether a particular property might be suitable for their client, and included in this assessment such factors as possible shortfall payments, and what sort of people the client may have to share with. Schemes also made a judgement on the landlord's suitability to take a client. This assessment included whether the landlord was flexible about untidiness and noise, and if the landlord had any experience with dealing with clients who might be disruptive.

▶   Schemes aimed at establishing sustainable tenancies, which meant that properties were often vetted, attempts were sometimes made to negotiate the rent down, and checks were made to ensure that legally binding tenancy agreements had been signed. Analysis of how these services were delivered in practice showed that schemes' attempts to vet properties were sometimes undermined by clients' willingness to live in sub-standard properties; landlords were thought to be unwilling to negotiate on rents, but were more likely to negotiate on the level of the shortfall; and landlords seemed happy for schemes to be involved in the legal side of the tenancy.

Chapter six: help with deposits

▶   There were four elements which comprised help with bond payments: completing furniture inventories; offering assistance with the deposit payment; helping the client to save to cover the cost of the deposit; and dealing with the end of tenancies. Few schemes offered only one approach to dealing with deposits: most tended to offer a mix of strategies.

▶   Seventy-seven per cent of schemes always or sometimes ensured that a furniture inventory was signed. Almost all the schemes giving financial help with guarantees completed inventories to protect their funds against false claims from landlords. Other types of scheme also completed inventories, however, as a service to clients to protect their deposits, and so perhaps enable them to transfer the deposit from one property to another.

▶   Eighty-one per cent of schemes gave some assistance with the deposit payment, which included negotiation, cash payment or guarantee payment. Many schemes also tried negotiation even if they gave financial assistance, although it was acknowledged that reliance on negotiation alone often meant that clients could only get access to lower-quality accommodation.

▶   Just over a quarter of schemes gave cash help with deposits, but it was evident that the establishment of schemes giving this type of help has been less common over the last few years, especially given the relative popularity of guarantee schemes. Most cash help was given in the form of a loan to cover the deposit given to either the landlord or the client. Schemes reported difficulties in recovering the loan at the end of the tenancy.

▶   Two fifths of schemes giving help with deposits did so by issuing guarantees. Most of the guarantee schemes were covering 30 clients or less, and issued guarantees with an average value of £242 each. All the guarantees covered damage, and most covered theft. Less than half the guarantees covered rent arrears and rent in lieu of notice. Three quarters of the schemes offered renewable guarantees.

▸ There was a wide variety in the type of guarantees offered, as illustrated by the case study schemes: some could be limited both financially and in terms of contingencies covered, and others could cover a wide range of eventualities.

▸ Some schemes helped clients to save money to pay for the deposit for the time after which the schemes' coverage would be withdrawn. Schemes helping clients in this way thought that this approach increased clients willingness to make the tenancy succeed. This approach did, however, increase schemes' administrative tasks with respect to checking payments into savings schemes.

▸ Nearly half the schemes giving no help with the payment of deposit money still gave indirect assistance with bonds by negotiating with the client's ex-landlord for the repayment of deposits from a previous tenancy.

▸ Schemes were usually involved in the ending of tenancies when they had issued guarantees. On average, schemes each dealt with eight claims a year, with each having an average value of £180. In all, 10 per cent of guarantee funds were paid out in claims. Schemes tended not to pursue clients for compensation, but did not offer help to these clients again.

Chapter seven: help with housing benefit and rent in advance

▸ A scheme's ability to help with rent in advance was often dependent on its involvement with the housing benefit application: one of the more common approaches to help with rent in advance was to negotiate away this requirement on the strength of offering services which speeded up housing benefit processing.

▸ Almost all schemes gave some sort of assistance with housing benefit, and four types of help were defined: assistance in completing the application form; making sure that the housing benefit cheque would be sent to the landlord; operating a 'fast-track' agreement with the housing benefit office; and continued liaison with the housing benefit office if the application was delayed.

▸ Not all schemes gave all types of help. Nearly half the schemes gave initial help with the application and then continued liaison with the housing benefit office;

and nearly half the schemes gave initial help with the application and then operated a fast-track housing benefit process.

▶ Extended help with housing benefit was not always necessary, since in some areas the benefit was processed within the statutory time period of two weeks.

▶ Eighty-nine schemes gave some sort of help with rent in advance. Four types of help were defined: application to the social fund; negotiation with the landlord to reduce or waive the requirement; making a single cash payment of rent in advance; and paying the rent until the housing benefit was processed.

▶ Negotiation with the landlord was the most popular strategy, and schemes most reliant on this approach were those most likely to have set up fast-track housing benefit systems, to enable them to bargain with the landlord on the strength of a quicker benefit payment.

▶ Local authority schemes were more than twice as likely as voluntary sector schemes to be giving single cash payments of rent in advance, but voluntary sector schemes more frequently made rent payments until the housing benefit had been processed.

▶ Some schemes offered rent payments since they considered that this was the only way in which they could persuade landlords to take on scheme clients. This might especially be the case in an area where landlords did not have a history of letting to people on low incomes.

Chapter eight: tenancy support

▶ Most of the schemes offered continued help both to the tenant and the landlord after the start of the tenancy, to ensure that the tenancies were sustained. This report refers to this sort of help as 'tenancy support'.

▶ Voluntary sector schemes were more likely to offer tenancy support than local authority schemes, and the variance was thought to rest on the fact that local authority schemes might consider such visits unnecessary since they were placing clients, who were unlikely to have support needs, in good quality accommodation where the landlords had been vetted relatively rigorously.

▶ Taken together, the majority of schemes continued to visit the tenant after the start of the tenancy. A distinction should be made between the sort of help schemes were giving, and resettlement work. Schemes themselves did not consider that they were giving specialised resettlement advice, and would refer clients needing such help on to another agency. Rather, scheme help tended to be concentrated on making sure that clients had settled into a tenancy.

▶ Help given during this initial period often included assistance in moving possessions; financial advice including help with budgeting; and perhaps a short series of visits which would finish once it was clear that the client no longer needed help.

▶ Some schemes also offered support to the landlord, which might include giving advice, sending out information packs, offering training, and giving advice on planning applications. The case study schemes had little involvement with landlord support, and their comments highlighted the possibility that giving landlord support might involve the scheme in cases of split loyalties.

▶ Some schemes were involved in tenancies which had come to an end, although only one of the case study schemes said that it made a point of trying to find out why tenancies were ending, and so angling its assistance towards resolving any disputes which may have arisen.

▶ Just over 90 per cent of schemes said that they always or sometimes found their clients somewhere else to live if a scheme tenancy had terminated. Giving this sort of help was usually dependent on the reason for the tenancy having come to an end: clients who had caused difficulties were unlikely to be helped a second time.

Chapter nine: clients

▶ Thirty-nine clients from five case study schemes were also interviewed as part of the evaluation. Most of the clients had come into contact with a scheme at a time of housing insecurity rather than in being in a more desperate situation of actual rooflessness. Many had, for example, been living in hostels or other types of temporary housing. Most of the clients had been helped into self-contained flats or houses, and the majority had been living in the accommodation for between seven and 12 months at the time of the interview.

▸ Clients' response to individual services was mixed. Clients expected that help given with finding somewhere to live would include the scheme either directly vetting the property or assisting the clients in defining what standards were acceptable.

▸ Although many of the clients felt confident about negotiating the rent themselves, help given with checking and understanding the tenancy agreement was appreciated. Clients did not often consider schemes' completion of tenancy agreements to be particularly helpful.

▸ All the clients needing help with deposits were given assistance. Almost all were happy with the help they were given, even if it included them having to make some sort of financial contribution.

▸ Most of the case study schemes negotiated with the landlord with respect to rent in advance payments, or directed clients towards landlords unlikely to ask for large sums of money. Clients were often unaware that this sort of help had been given, although most commented that they were able to afford the rent in advance the landlord had asked for.

▸ Clients were particularly appreciative of help with housing benefit, including help with filling in the form and especially help with dealing with large shortfalls between the housing benefit payable and the rent charged. Clients' uncertainties about being able to deal with budgeting once tenancies had started indicated that perhaps more help could be offered in this area.

▸ A third of the clients said that they would have liked help in moving possessions, and some clients moving into unfurnished tenancies said that they would have liked some assistance with acquiring furniture and kitchen equipment.

▸ Clients with limited experience of renting privately, and using a scheme which did not offer tenancy support visits, said that they would have liked the scheme to have made sure that they were settling in, and that there were no problems. Many clients considered visits beyond this initial period to be unnecessary.

▸ The majority of clients said that they felt able to go to the scheme if any difficulties arose with the tenancy. Many of the clients commented, however, that they did not think that such a circumstance would arise, and that they felt fairly confident about dealing with such eventualities themselves.

▶ Client's evaluation of scheme help in general terms showed that the aspect of schemes which was most appreciated was not a definable single service, but schemes' being supportive during an obviously stressful time.

▶ The group of services which was considered most important was any help given with deposit payments. Almost all the clients given this sort of help said that they would not have been able to secure their tenancy without it.

▶ Although 27 of the clients were satisfied with the tenancies which had been secured, 28 clients said that they intended to move. Twelve of these clients were dissatisfied with the standard of the accommodation. Other clients said they would move if a council or housing association tenancy became available. The majority of clients evidently considered that the schemes' helping them into private sector tenancies constituted a short-to-medium-term solution to their housing need.

Chapter ten: landlords

▶ Forty-three landlords were interviewed, who had had some involvement with one of the five case study schemes: either the landlords had used the scheme to find tenants, or the landlord had had a tenant who used the scheme to help make an advance payment. Most of the landlords were 'sideline' landlords, and let to supplement their main income. Between them, the landlords had 519 lets, and were letting to a total of 94 tenants from a scheme.

▶ Each group of landlords had particular characteristics. Landlords associated with the London scheme tended to let only one furnished property, and all had been letting for less than five years. The Charity Scheme landlords included three managing agents, and had clearly had a greater experience of letting. Most of the Westerbury Scheme managers had let property for under five years, but the landlords tended to have a larger number of lettings than the London Scheme landlords. The Metropolitan Scheme landlords were similar to the Westerbury landlords, but included some landlords with lets in shared houses. The County Scheme landlords almost all offered lets in shared accommodation.

▶ Making distinctions between the landlord types was important, since responses to scheme services differed amongst the landlord groups. The landlords operating towards the bottom end of the market, in shared properties, valued schemes' ability to supply tenants. By comparison, the landlords offering more self-contained accommodation said that they could find tenants quite easily, and so would not actively seek tenants from a scheme. All landlords, however, considered that a schemes' usefulness rested on whether clients were being vetted before they were passed on to landlords.

- Most of the landlords said that they had in the past negotiated on the level of the rent, although few said that the scheme had tried to negotiate. The only exception was London landlords, who said that the scheme had told them what rent to charge. The landlords were unhappy that the rent was set at a level below the market average.

- Landlords were largely indifferent to whether schemes had any involvement with the tenancy agreement, although some landlords with more limited experience of letting were grateful in cases where schemes had taken over responsibility for this aspect of setting up the tenancy.

- Most of the landlords were indifferent to the idea of schemes completing furniture inventories. Even the landlords with furnished lets often did not complete inventories, since they thought that it was unnecessary. Only one of the landlords who had a furniture inventory completed by the scheme considered this service beneficial.

- Almost all the landlords charged some sort of deposit, although the majority said that they would in certain circumstances waive, reduce or accept the deposit in instalments. However, few of the schemes had tried to negotiate the deposit down. Landlords with properties at the lower end of the market were evidently more open to the idea of negotiating the deposit than landlords further up the market.

- Deposit guarantees were given to 14 of the landlords, four of whom said that they would have preferred cash. There was also some objection to the type of guarantee issued: landlords of the Westerbury Scheme, for example, were critical of the guarantee only covering damage, and not covering rent in arrears or rent in lieu of notice. Most of the landlords were happy with the guarantees, however, and many of the landlords not getting guarantees said that they would be prepared to accept one.

- Only one of the schemes gave cash help with rent in advance: the Charity Scheme paid the rent until the housing benefit was processed. Most of the landlords said that the scheme had not approached them with respect to negotiation on rent in advance. Almost all the landlords said that they had in the past waived or reduced this requirement, if they were certain that they would be paid housing benefit.

▶   Landlords with less experience of housing benefit were more appreciative of help
    with the process of application. Landlords with more experience were indifferent
    to whether the scheme was involved or not.

▶   Landlords were equivocal about schemes' continuing to visit clients after a
    tenancy had been established. Thirteen landlords did not consider the visits to be
    particularly beneficial, but 13 considered that the visits were good for the tenant,
    and so of benefit to the tenancy. Some landlords thought that schemes did not
    visit frequently enough. These were landlords with limited experience of letting
    to people on housing benefit, and who had taken on scheme tenants on the
    assumption that the scheme would 'police' the tenancy.

▶   Few of the landlords said that they took advantage of any advice and support
    which the scheme might offer them. Most considered that advice from the scheme
    was a service for the clients' benefit only.

▶   Not all the landlords were satisfied with the way in which the scheme had dealt
    with the end of the tenancy. Seven of the landlords who had had clients covered
    by written guarantees said that the tenancy had ended badly, with respect to the
    landlord having lost money which the guarantee would not cover.

▶   In discussing landlords' assessment of schemes' good points, two groupings
    emerged. Landlords at the bottom end of the market were happy with schemes
    providing a supply of tenants. Landlords further up the market were happiest with
    the Charity Scheme, which offered rent payments until the housing benefit was
    processed.

Conclusion: the role and delivery of access help

▶   The role of access help was best defined not as a solution to rooflessness, but a
    preventative measure enabling clients to avoid having to move through a series
    of insecure housing situations, risking rooflessness in the process.

▶   A list of best practice points was given, which acknowledged the diversity of help
    given with access.

▶   Schemes often tailored their services to the peculiarities of the niche rental market
    they were aiming at and to the needs of the clients they were helping. The
    findings from the case study schemes showed that most access help constituted

a valuable, and valued, response to the difficulties clients faced in attempting to secure accommodation in the private rented sector. Of particular importance, however, was giving financial assistance with advance payments. This sort of help meant that the search process became much easier, because clients then had access to a larger choice of properties. Schemes were also able to use advance payments as a means of securing better-quality accommodation for their clients.

Introduction

Access schemes

The development of schemes helping people secure access to accommodation in the private rented sector has been a noticeable feature of the voluntary sector and local authority response to homelessness in recent years. These schemes offer a range of services which might include help with rent in advance, dealing with deposits by giving cash or a guarantee, and managing accommodation registers to help people find places to stay. The usefulness of these types of schemes has been endorsed by the government. Since 1990, the s73 grant programme has been giving individual grants to voluntary sector agencies helping homeless people and in 1994/5 specifically targeted its funds at agencies offering accommodation registers (Department of the Environment, 1995a). In 1995, a general consent was published, allowing local authorities to pay rent in advance, give deposit guarantees, and indemnify landlords for 'specified losses and expenses' arising from a particular tenancy (Department of the Environment, 1995b).

Despite the general agreement that assistance given to secure tenancies is a valuable development, there has been little consensus on how such help should be delivered. For example, all rent in advance and deposit schemes help clients secure a property by dealing with the requirement to pay bonds or rent up front - a sum of money which may be hundreds of pounds. The way in which this objective can be met varies, however, and can include giving the client a repayable loan; giving the client a grant; or offering to the landlord a guarantee in place of the actual payment. In addition to meeting these advance costs, some schemes offer associated services, such as inventory checks in furnished accommodation, or paying the rent until the housing benefit comes through.

Similarly, accommodation registers can be defined at a basic level as agencies giving clients information on vacancies in the private rented sector. The means by which this help is given varies, however. The scheme might actually help the client in the process of looking, by introducing landlords and taking the client to view properties. Alternatively, the help might simply include compiling a list of vacancies which the clients themselves then use to contact landlords. Again as with rent in advance or deposit schemes, registers sometimes offer a range of other services including help with applying for housing benefit and continued support once a tenancy starts.

Thus one rent in advance scheme, deposit scheme or accommodation register can differ radically from another. In addition, there is a degree of overlap between the types of scheme. For example, all three might vet landlords to assess the standard and suitability of their property for a particular client, and all three might try and generate a better choice of accommodation for their clients by liaising with landlords in their area. The high degree of variety and overlap seems to indicate that distinctions between the types of scheme are to some degree artificial. This report acknowledges the similarities between the schemes by referring to them all as 'access schemes', since they all facilitate access to accommodation.

The basis of evaluation

This report is based on research into access schemes operating in England and Wales, and is aimed at informing housing and homelessness practitioners of possible access help options, and the advantages, disadvantages and constraints attached to taking different approaches. The research had two key objectives: to gain a clearer impression of the nature of access schemes currently operating; and to complete an evaluation of those schemes. Quantitative methods have been applied to the more descriptive task of defining schemes' essential characteristics and the services offered. The evaluation of schemes, by contrast, has been carried out using qualitative analysis. Initially it was considered that the evaluation would comprise a assessment of schemes' cost-effectiveness. However, as the research progressed, it became clear that this approach was not suitable. It would have been possible to derive conclusions on the cost-effectiveness of individual access schemes, but comparing costs between schemes would not have been entirely appropriate: schemes were not dealing with clients with similar support needs, the delivery of services was by no means uniform, and the effectiveness of each scheme was very much dependent on the characteristics of their local rental market. Any conclusions drawn from this sort of research would have rested on a series of generalised assumptions and simplifications - interesting in methodological terms, but perhaps of limited value to the practitioner.

Rather than taking a quantitative approach, therefore, the evaluation has been qualitative. Help with access has been analysed by using material collected in interviews with scheme managers, landlords and clients. The scheme manager interviews have enabled some analysis of the rationale underpinning different approaches to access help, drawing out the perceived advantages and disadvantages of delivering particular services. Crucially, the report compares scheme managers' views on access help with landlords' experience of access schemes, and clients views on the help they received. The evaluation has therefore rested on the self-assessment of project managers and the opinions of service users. Using this method of evaluation, the study has been able to identify the key essentials of help with access, and highlight areas of good practice.

Methods

The research methods had four components: a postal survey of schemes; interviews with scheme managers; interviews with clients who had found accommodation through using schemes; and interviews with landlords who were currently involved with or had had some involvement with schemes.

Postal survey

There was no centralised information from which to choose schemes to include in the postal survey, which meant that a survey sample had to be created. A call for information on individual schemes was circulated in the housing press, and through internal newsletters to Citizens' Advice Bureaux and Shelter offices. Contacts made by Quaker Social Action through the publication of the *Rent Guarantee Scheme Handbook* were also followed up. In addition, the sample included all the projects currently funded under the s73 grant programme with performance indicators for accommodation register management.

Information was gathered on over 200 schemes, to which strict criteria were applied on the exact definition of an access scheme. All schemes included in the research had to fit four criteria: they had to help people in housing need; the tenancy was to be independent of long-term support; the accommodation had to be in the private rented sector; and the tenancies were intended to last for at least six months. Applying these criteria reduced the number of scheme contacts, since it excluded projects which placed the majority of their clients in council or housing association tenancies; emergency or nightstop projects, which placed clients for one or two nights only; outreach projects which referred their clients to hostels; and projects dealing with clients whose needs require the client to have lifelong support. Schemes such as private sector leasing schemes (PSL) and housing associations as managing agents (HAMA) were also excluded since they entail the organisation actually taking over control of the property and managing it on behalf of the landlord - a process which brings forward slightly different issues than the operation of the majority of access schemes.

The final list of contacts was something under 200 schemes. This selection was not strictly representative, since it did not include many of the newer schemes being set up at the time when contacts were being made. Rather, the final sample arrived at presents a 'snapshot' of a broad selection of schemes operating in February and March 1995. Although there was no intention for the survey sample to be representative, some biases in the sample should be noted. There is an obvious over-representation of schemes receiving s73 funding. In addition, there is a slight bias in the selection towards the more rural areas. Only 22 per cent of the schemes were in local authorities in either London or in other metropolitan areas; and 22 per cent of schemes were in local authorities defined as mixed urban/rural or deep rural. There is, however, a reasonable geographic spread amongst schemes throughout England and Wales. None of the schemes which were included operated on a national basis.

All the schemes which were contacted were sent a questionnaire in February 1995. A total of 161 schemes responded. The questionnaire asked schemes about the nature of their organisation; staffing; their funding arrangements; the way in which they took on clients; the application of criteria for taking on landlords; the services offered; and the frequency with which they experienced particular problems. The schemes were also asked to specify any other problems they might have, and to give any additional comment. It should be noted that funding and client details were asked of the financial year 1993/4, which meant that information from schemes established after April 1993 was limited slightly.

Interviews with scheme managers

Semi-structured interviews took place with 11 scheme managers, of schemes chosen to represent a variety of approaches taken to help with access. The schemes included eight voluntary sector schemes, two local authority housing department schemes, and one housing association scheme. Four of the schemes helped clients find accommodation, but gave no cash assistance with access costs, and the remaining seven gave cash help or guarantees to cover deposits. One of these schemes also gave loans to cover the cost of the rent until the first housing benefit payment was made. To protect their confidentiality, the schemes have been given pseudonyms. A brief description of each of the schemes is given in appendix one. Project managers were asked about the organisational context in which their scheme operated; its financial structure and long-term financial strategies; how it dealt with clients and landlords, and why such approaches were taken; how particular services were delivered, and the rationale for deciding which services to offer; and the way in which they themselves evaluated their scheme.

Interviews with clients

Five of the eleven schemes were chosen as 'case study' schemes, which meant that semi-structured interviews also took place with clients and landlords. Schemes were asked to provide a representative list of the clients, ten of whom were chosen at random for interview. In all, 39 interviews were achieved. Some difficulties were encountered in interviewing clients who had used the Metropolitan Scheme, since it did not keep contact with the clients who had used its weekly list of vacancies. Appendix two gives tables summarising clients' characteristics. The clients were asked about their circumstances on first contacting the scheme, their housing history, and the nature of their current tenancy. The remainder of the interview was taken up with questions about the process of looking for and securing private rented accommodation and settling into their tenancy, and how the scheme had helped in that process. Clients were also asked to assess how important the scheme had been in securing them their accommodation, and which was the most important help that could be made available to anyone in housing need looking for somewhere to stay.

Interviews with landlords

Semi-structured interviews also took place with landlords who had either used the scheme to find tenants, or whose tenants had used the scheme to provide advance payments. Again schemes were asked to provide a list of landlords they had used in the past or were currently using, and ten landlords from each list were chosen at random for interview over the telephone. In total, 43 interviews were achieved. Appendix three gives tables detailing the landlords' characteristics.

The landlords were asked about the number and nature of properties they let, ways in which they found tenants, and how they set up and terminated tenancies. There were a number of questions contrasting the landlords' experiences of letting with and without the involvement of the scheme. Landlords were also asked whether they would consider paying for scheme services.

The structure of the report

The first section of the report contains four chapters which present a largely narrative description of access schemes, derived from postal survey data. The section begins with a chapter which introduces the issue of access, and sets out the policy context informing the establishment of access schemes. Chapter two looks at the development, status and funding of schemes, and concludes that the status of a scheme - as being operated by either a voluntary sector or local authority - had important implications for its funding position. Chapter three looks in detail at the way in which schemes dealt with clients in terms of the number of clients helped, restrictions imposed, and referral processes. Again differences emerged between schemes according to their status, and according to their scheme type in terms of whether or not help was given with deposits. The final chapter in the section looks at schemes' dealings with landlords. This chapter demonstrates again that scheme status and scheme type had an impact - in this respect on both the schemes' relationship with landlords, and on their use of different types of accommodation.

The second section of the report contains four chapters which look at the help being offered by access schemes. The wide range of services is ordered into four groups: help with finding somewhere to live; help with deposits; help with housing benefit and rent in advance; and tenancy support. Each chapter of the section highlights the different approaches to service delivery. A degree of evaluation is introduced in this section; the chapters discuss schemes' decisions on the help that should be given, possible constraints which operated on such an approach, and the perceived advantages and disadvantages.

The third section of the report continues the evaluation. Chapters nine and ten present help with access from the point of view of clients and landlords. The chapters discuss responses to particular scheme services, and clients' and landlords' assessments of schemes' good and bad points.

The report's conclusion defines more clearly what role access help may best serve. The conclusion then offers a series of good practice points.

Section One:

Access Schemes,
Their Clients and Landlords

Advance payments

Although people in housing need face a range of difficulties in trying to secure accommodation, the requirement to pay rent in advance and deposit or bond money appears as one of the more consistent barriers. The 1993/4 Survey of English Housing found that 73 per cent of tenants had made payments of rent in advance, and 63 per cent a deposit or non-returnable fee (Carey, 1995). Similar findings were presented in the 1994 study of the lower end of the private rented sector in Glasgow, which revealed that 70 per cent of the sample had paid a bond, rent in advance or both to secure their present accommodation. The people in the survey living in housing in multiple occupation, for example, had paid an average of £148 rent in advance and £118 in bond money (Kemp and Rhodes, 1994). For people on limited incomes with no savings, this requirement constitutes a sometimes insuperable barrier to securing accommodation. A 1990 survey of housing need in Cardiff found that over half the people interviewed said that it was difficult to find accommodation because of the need to pay a deposit, and nearly a third said that they could not afford to pay rent in advance (Bailey, 1992). The qualitative study of people moving whilst on housing benefit also came to similar conclusions, as many of its respondents said that the requirement to pay deposits or rent in advance restricted their choice of places to stay (Kemp *et al.*, 1994).

Most of the access scheme clients who were interviewed considered finding advance payments to be a big factor in deciding whether or not they could take a particular property. Many had turned down accommodation because they did not have money to pay, and had lost the chance of getting places they had thought suitable: '*it takes you ages to save up and by that time the flats have gone*'. There was some degree of exasperation amongst the clients in talking about this requirement: landlords asked for substantial amounts of money from people who evidently could not afford it:

> *Obviously people who go for flats are on the Social, they haven't got a few hundred pounds. It speaks for itself doesn't it?*
> (Client, County Scheme)

> *I just can't understand how people can say they'll take people that are unemployed as tenants, but they want x amount up front. If you're unemployed, you're obviously scrimping and saving because of what you get...Why the hell don't they just say, 'Sorry, no DSS people'?*
> (Client, Southwest Scheme)

Finding money for the deposit was considered particularly problematic. Twenty-six of the clients said that bond payments were a big factor in their housing decisions. In some cases, having to make these payments was one of the major barriers to getting somewhere to live:

> *Well, I can see the landlord or landlady's point of view, but the deposit,*
> *on the whole, if you've got nothing, is very difficult to find...I'd say it was*
> *probably the biggest nuisance of the lot of it, bar the DSS stuff.*
>   (Client, Westerbury Scheme)

For some people, finding deposit money was the biggest problem of all: *'that's what stops people from getting places to live'.*

Fewer clients (20) said that finding money for rent in advance was a factor in getting somewhere to stay. The relative ease probably reflected the fact that in two of the case study areas it was common to get loans from the social fund to meet these payments. Even where this was the case, however, the client had to consider whether the fund would pay out on a given rent:

> *They'll ask for four weeks' rent in advance, and sometimes the rent might*
> *be £85 a week, or £95, and there's no way the Social will give you that*
> *£400 because they'll say 'No, it's too high'. So you can be left in limbo-*
> *land.*
>   (Client, Metropolitan Scheme)

Furthermore, the social fund was considered to be slow in making its decisions, which meant that the client might lose that property if the landlord was unwilling to wait.

So, for the majority of the clients, making advance payments was a key barrier to securing accommodation. Some were able to pay by getting a loan from either relatives or the social fund, which meant that tenancies started in debt. Also, these loans enabled them to pay either the deposit or the rent in advance but usually not both. Rather than facing this sort of debt, most clients instead tried to find places where no advance payment was required, which - as will be seen in a later section - substantially narrowed down the choice of accommodation.

Attitude of landlords

A further difficulty faced by people on low incomes who want to rent privately is the unwillingness of many landlords to let to people on housing benefit. A number of reports have highlighted this problem: for example, a report on the lower end of the private rented sector in Glasgow found that unemployed people were the type of tenant least preferred by landlords (Kemp and Rhodes, 1994); and a smaller-scale qualitative study of private landlords found that most did not want to let to people out of work (Bevan *et al.*, 1995).

The tenant's view was reflected in a qualitative study of people moving whilst on housing benefit. All the renting respondents in the study felt that being on benefit put them at a disadvantage in looking for accommodation: one of the respondents said of landlords, *'nine out of ten say no DHSS and no housing benefit'* (Kemp *et al.*, 1994). This prejudice was also a problem encountered by some of the access scheme clients. One client mentioned why he thought landlords were unwilling to let to himself and his friend:

> *they wouldn't take us because we're not working, a lot of them. Well, 99 per cent of landlords won't take you because you're on housing benefit, because they're waiting for the money.*
>
> (Client, Metropolitan Scheme)

Clearly therefore, people in housing need find it difficult to secure accommodation because some landlords do not like having to deal with the housing benefit process. In some cases, this view was compounded by generally negative opinions of people who had been homeless (Bevan, *et al.*, 1995).

Quality

Another barrier to securing housing in the private rented sector was the limited availability of places to rent that were in reasonable condition. According to the 1991 English House Condition Survey, an average of 20 per cent of dwellings in the private rented sector was unfit, compared with 6 per cent of owner occupied and 7 per cent of local authority housing (Green and Hansbro, 1995). According to many of the access scheme clients interviewed, looking for somewhere to stay could entail an extensive search through any number of poor quality properties, trying to assess which was the least bad. One of the clients had looked at *'All the tat in* [this town]' before getting somewhere reasonable. Another client had also seen some poor quality properties:

> *Some of the places me and my husband had been looking at were horrible and it was 'Eeeuuughhhh'. You know, you wouldn't let pigs never mind humans live in there. So it has been a battle between finding places like that and some not wanting people on the Social or you had to be working.*
>
> (Client, Metropolitan Scheme)

There was, to some extent, a trade off being made by some clients, in accepting poorer quality accommodation where access was easier rather than hold out for somewhere more salubrious, but where access would necessitate payments of high advance costs. Thus for some tenants, it was possible to find accommodation were the rent was reasonable, where advance payments were not required, and where the landlord was willing to let to housing benefit claimants, but at the cost of living in substandard accommodation.

Finding somewhere

So far, a number of factors have been discussed which prevent people from securing access to accommodation in the private sector. Together, the barriers present a sort of obstacle course which clients often find impossible to complete. One client said that, looking through the newspapers for accommodation, all he saw was: *'"Deposit", "Deposit", "No DSS", "Deposit", "No DSS", which seems kind of depressing'*. Another noted that there was *'always a snag that you couldn't get somewhere. So it has been a struggle really'*. These things add together to create a situation where people on low incomes find securing rented accommodation problematic. The study of the lower end of the private rented sector in Glasgow, the majority of a sample of tenants, boarders and hostel residents (69 per cent) agreed with the statement that 'it is very difficult to find accommodation these days' (Kemp and Rhodes, 1994).

The problems are intensified to some degree by the avoidance strategies taken by many tenants in dealing with individual obstacles. They spend time looking for landlords willing to let to people on housing benefit, and they try and find places where deposit and rent in advance are not asked for. Of the 26 scheme clients who had rented before, only six had paid a deposit at their last rented place, and eight had paid rent in advance. These strategies, however, considerably reduce the range of rented accommodation they can secure, and make the process of searching for somewhere more protracted and hence more expensive. Furthermore, the limited choice available can sometimes leave them in poor quality properties not particularly well suited to their household's needs.

The policy response

The problems faced by people in housing need trying to gain access to private rented accommodation have been acknowledged in initiatives at national, statutory, level as well as at the level of localised voluntary sector response. In particular, two forms of assistance have emerged as being of importance: compiling accommodation registers, and help with advance payments. Both local authorities and voluntary sector housing organisations have become involved in offering both sorts of help. The remainder of this chapter will discuss the background of each type of scheme, and briefly introduces the sort of help given.

Accommodation registers

Schemes compiling accommodation registers are able to sidestep many aspects of difficulties with access. They can offer clients properties of an appropriate type, where the rent and quality is reasonable, and where there is a certainty that the landlord is willing to let to benefit recipients. The importance of this sort of scheme has been consistently acknowledged by the government. In 1989, the Department of the Environment's review of homelessness legislation singled out the establishment of accommodation registers as being a particularly significant development, which it intended to support:

> The Government proposes to encourage a greater supply [of accommodation] through publicity and through help to voluntary bodies engaged in promoting or organising lodgings. Registers of lodgings available are important and local authorities will be encouraged to co-operate with voluntary agencies to establish them, especially in the 'pressure areas'.
>
> (Department of the Environment, 1989)

This support was reiterated two years later, in 1991, when the government stressed that one of its homelessness policy initiatives was the funding of voluntary sector agencies helping people to find temporary or permanent accommodation (*Hansard*, 17 Jan 1991). This funding was available through the s73 grant programme, one of the primary objectives of which has been the funding of schemes managing accommodation registers.

Despite the consensus that accommodation registers fulfil an invaluable function, there seems to have been no agreement as to what services should be offered. There has been no published research completed on accommodation registers, although an unpublished report for the Department of the Environment, evaluating the s73 grant programme, did include some findings on the way different registers funded by the programme operated (Bevan *et al.*, 1994). All registers offered basic help facilitating a match between tenant and landlord, but the ways in which this matching was done, and the range of associated services, differed tremendously. For example, some registers operated an extensive list of properties which was updated regularly, and to which the client was able to refer in the search for somewhere to stay. Other registers spent less time generating and updating vacancy lists, and operated more to support the client through a search process and through the first months of the tenancy. Furthermore, many schemes offered additional services beyond the basic matching function. These included assistance with access costs; helping the client make housing benefit and/or social fund applications; and advising the landlord on tenancy legislation.

Help with advance payments

Because the issues surrounding rent in advance and bonds differ slightly, each will be discussed separately.

Rent in advance

For people in receipt of income support, it is possible to get help with rent in advance from the social fund. Indeed, the Social Security Advisory Committee Report of 1992 recommended that 'loans should be made available...for the payment of rent in advance', since it acknowledged that people on income support 'frequently have no resources with which to pay large sums for advance rent' (Social Security Advisory Committee, 1992). It is assumed that the payment of retrospective housing benefit will enable the applicant to pay off the loan, although in some cases the rent in advance is given as a grant.

However, there is some ground for believing that few people approach the social fund for help with advance rent, and that the success rate is limited. A large-scale report evaluating the social fund, published in 1992, demonstrated that fewer than one per cent of applications to the fund in its sample area were for rent in advance (Huby and Dix, 1992). In 1990-91, 10,300 loans were paid to cover rent in advance (Saunders, 1991), but evidence suggests that many more apply for assistance and are unsuccessful. For example, the study of the lower end of the private sector in Glasgow revealed that only seven per cent of people in its survey (who had moved since 1988) had applied to the social fund. Within this small group, the success rate was low: two thirds of the applicants had been refused, and only one quarter of applicants had received a loan or grant, with the majority then getting a loan (Kemp and Rhodes, 1994).

Because of these specific problems, schemes exist which offer help with rent in advance. There is little information available on the early development of such schemes since, unlike accommodation registers and bond guarantee schemes, they have had - until the issue of the general consent in 1995 - no consistent or organised 'backing' from government or voluntary agencies. Although it is a separate service, help with rent in advance is usually linked with help with deposits, and schemes offering only a rent in advance service have received little attention.

There is perhaps less variety in the way in which these schemes operate than in other sorts of access project. In the case of local authorities, some have set aside a specific fund from which loans for rent in advance can be given, with the requirement that the first housing benefit cheque be paid directly back into the fund. Some local authorities also offer to the landlord the additional service of a 'fast-tracked' housing benefit payment, which speeds up their tenant's initial application. Voluntary sector schemes can make similar arrangements, paying rent in advance on behalf of their client from a lump sum of cash donated from local churches or charities, and making arrangements for repayment from the first housing benefit cheque. Both schemes may also choose to continue offering to pay the rent to the landlord until the housing benefit application is processed and the first payment made.

Bonds

The issues surrounding the payment of bonds differ from those associated with rent in advance. An assumption is sometimes made that tenants need only transfer their bond from one tenancy to another, and that specific assistance is not required. It is not always the case, however, that tenants can easily recover their bond from a landlord once the tenancy has terminated. The government itself acknowledged this issue in January 1995, in a written answer to the Commons: 'we are aware that problems with the return of deposits sometimes arise', but noted that no national figures were available (*Hansard*, 19th Jan 1995). A survey conducted by the National Consumer Council in 1990 revealed that one in four tenants had had their deposit unfairly retained by the landlord (*Inside Housing*, 2 Mar. 1990). The study of people moving whilst on housing benefit explored the deposit issue in more detail. More than half the small sample interviewed had their last deposit retained by the landlord. Only three had been able to pay for their current deposit by using a deposit returned from the last tenancy; the majority had borrowed from friends or family to meet the requirement (Kemp *et al.*, 1994).

Many commentators would see that difficulties with bonds as being a direct consequence of the changes to the old single payments scheme which were made through the introduction of the social fund in 1988. Before 1988, a claimant could apply for a single payment to cover the cost of a returnable bond. However, reliance on this system had been heavy, and use had increased rapidly. By 1986-7, expenditure had reached £6.1m, with deposits averaging £150 each (Saunders, 1991). In addition, it was claimed that the system had been abused by both landlords and tenants. For these reasons, single payments to cover bonds were scrapped when changes were introduced in 1988: the new social fund regulations made no allowance for such help. As a consequence, some schemes have been established which offer cash assistance with bonds - sometimes as a loan, which the scheme recovers from the landlord or tenant at the end of the tenancy.

In 1990 the National Consumer Council (NCC) initiated a campaign which highlighted what it saw as the need for a national bond board, similar to the board established in New

South Wales. There deposits are paid to the board rather than to the landlord and the tenant has the assurance that, should no claim arise, the deposit will be repaid quickly. The NCC gained a great deal of support for its proposals initially, and the government announced that it was considering a national scheme. The campaign lost momentum, but the government continued to express support of more limited local bond guarantee schemes, which sidestep the requirement to pay a deposit by offering to the landlord a written guarantee in its place.

In 1992, the government interest in this sort of scheme resulted in the setting up of a rent deposit project, to be administered by the Notting Hill Housing Trust, and funded under the Rough Sleeper Initiative. The Rent Deposit Fund was given a budget of £110,000 to cover deposits - either in the form of guarantees or cash payments - and funds to cover administrative and legal action costs. The report evaluating this and a limited number of other similar schemes concluded that in particular help given by issuing guarantees was 'extremely effective' and a 'growing and successful innovation', and that there was '...scope for centrally funded model schemes and for local authorities, housing associations and voluntary groups to set up local schemes' (Randall and Brown, 1994).

Since that time, the government has increasingly stressed the role local authorities might take in establishing bond guarantee boards, and finally in 1995 it issued 'general consent' for authorities to operate these schemes (*Hansard*, oral answers, 13 Feb.1995; DoE, 1995b).

The variety of approaches taken in giving help with deposits was highlighted by the Churches National Housing Coalition *Rent Guarantee Scheme Handbook*, (Jenn, 1994) which offered guidance to organisations hoping to offer this sort of help. The Handbook included a survey of twelve projects run by both local authorities and voluntary sector organisations. Although all projects offered bond guarantees, the value of the guarantees varied, as did the eventualities covered. Thus, some guarantees were set to the equivalent value of one month's rent, and others up to £100 or £200; and some guarantees covered damage only whilst others were for damage and theft. As with other access schemes, there was a range of associated services which was not uniformly provided by all schemes, including help with housing benefit applications and continuing support.

Conclusion

This chapter has explored the issue of access, by looking in more detail at the barriers facing people on low incomes wanting to secure access to the private rented sector. Problems of affordability, advance payments, the attitude of landlords, the condition of properties and the difficulties in actually finding appropriate accommodation were all highlighted. The policy response to access problems has largely concentrated on the development of accommodation registers and help with advance payments. Although there has been general recognition that such schemes are a necessary and useful response, there has not been a uniform structure to the patterns of services provided within each scheme type, or in the way those services are delivered.

Chapter Two
Access Schemes - Development, Status and Funding

Introduction

Chapter one demonstrated the range of difficulties with access, and responses to those difficulties in terms of the establishment of accommodation registers and schemes helping with advance payments. This chapter will look at access schemes themselves in more detail, using data from the postal questionnaire and from the interviews with scheme managers. In particular, the chapter will focus on schemes' chronological development, the status of their parent organisation, and the reasons why the schemes were established. Patterns of funding and future funding strategies will then be considered. The chapter will conclude by discussing the funds used to back the issue of deposit guarantees. The chapter will show that there are key differences between schemes established by voluntary sector agencies and those run by local authority housing departments.

Patterns of development

The data collected from the questionnaire show that the establishment of access schemes is a relatively recent phenomenon. Although the earliest established scheme in the sample was 1967, this was very much an exception: 90 per cent of the schemes were set up after 1990. As Table 2.1 shows, there were two surges of activity: in 1991 and 1993. In each of these years, scheme establishment was more than double that of the previous year.

The surge in activity in 1991 reflects the high number of s73-funded schemes in the sample. The growth of schemes in that year probably follows the changes to s73 funding which, for the first time from the beginning of 1990, made grants available to smaller individual projects. The doubling of schemes in 1993 was a consequence of an increase in the number of schemes offering deposit guarantees. The reason for the sudden popularity of this type of help may be the publication of further details about how such schemes might be set up. One deposit guarantee scheme manager commented that they had set up a scheme in response to the publication of the *Rent Guarantee Scheme Handbook* in 1993, which offered advice on the various approaches which may be taken to setting up such a scheme. Certainly, by 1994 interest in the publication had grown so far as to justify a reprint (Jenn, 1994). The government report giving a positive appraisal of a pilot guarantee scheme (Randall and Brown, 1994) may also have given encouragement to establish deposit schemes.

Table 2.1
Access schemes - year of establishment

	number	percentage
pre-1989	16	10
1990	9	6
1991	20	13
1992	20	13
1993	41	26
1994	43	27
1995 (to Feb.)	7	5
Total	156	100
Source: postal survey		

Schemes' organisational status

All the schemes fell into one of four 'status' categories. The majority of schemes, 90 (56 per cent), were charities or voluntary sector schemes. Although a small number of these were stand-alone schemes, most were being run by a larger voluntary sector agency. Forty-eight schemes (30 per cent) were run by local authorities - usually through the housing department's homelessness section. Fourteen schemes (nine per cent) were operated by housing associations. A small number of schemes (five per cent) were managed jointly by two or more types of organisation: usually a voluntary sector scheme working together with the social services, the probation department or with a housing association.

The majority of the access schemes extended and complemented work already being done to help a particular group of people in housing need. Beyond this generalisation, however, there was a great deal of diversity. Description of four of the case study schemes will illustrate this point.

▶ The Westerbury Scheme evolved from work being undertaken by a housing association in conjunction with the local council and the social services department, all three of which were involved in the running of a 10-bed hostel for young people. There were evident difficulties with securing move-on accommodation, and it was observed that not having money to pay deposits was the main drawback encountered. As a consequence a deposit fund was established using donations to the hostel, and the housing association started to issue written guarantees. At first the guarantees were only available to hostel residents, but this restriction was later relaxed and the guarantee was made available to other young people in housing need.

▶ The London Scheme operated within a local authority's homelessness section. The scheme emerged from concern over the high number of statutory homeless families in temporary accommodation in hostels and bed and breakfast hotels. The scheme located suitable accommodation in the private rented sector and negotiated with landlords to set up independent tenancies with no access costs. Households in temporary accommodation were then offered the tenancies, which were intended to last for at least 12 months.

▶ The Northwest Scheme operated as part of a nightstop project, which offered emergency shelter to young people. It was evident that assistance with more permanent accommodation was needed, since some young people were returning to the project on a regular basis. An accommodation register scheme was set up, and was integrated into the outreach and resettlement work being completed by the nightstop project.

▶ The Metropolitan Scheme operated within a welfare rights organisation, which also ran a hostel for young people. Initially, contacts with landlords were developed to help people move on from the hostel, but the high number of requests for help with finding accommodation at the shop-front offices led to the production of a weekly list of available vacancies, and the offering of help to contact landlords and sort out housing benefit claims.

All these examples illustrate schemes which were established following the recognition of a gap in a range of services already being delivered by the parent organisation. Help with access was integrated into those services and often complemented advice, outreach and resettlement work.

As has been mentioned, few of the schemes were divorced from the associated services of a 'parent' organisation. However, of the schemes where project managers were interviewed two were 'stand alone'.

▸ The Churches Scheme was set up through the joint working of a number of churches in a small town, which wanted to help homeless people in their area. Inspired by the *Rent Guarantee Scheme Handbook*, (Jenn, 1994) the decision was taken to set up a deposit fund against which written guarantees were issued. The scheme was run entirely by volunteers and offered no help finding accommodation or tenant support work. Rather, it was expected that agents referring the client to the scheme would give this sort of help.

▸ The Southwest Scheme was set up by an ex-Housing Corporation worker following recognition of the need for such help amongst non-statutory homeless people. Funds for the issue of guarantees were acquired from donations. The scheme took referrals from the local housing advice centre and was paid by the council to take up to 25 referrals from its homelessness section each year.

These sorts of 'stand alone' scheme, unless heavily financed, were perhaps more reliant on forging links with appropriate agencies to refer suitable clients and to deal with client support work.

Funding

The high degree of integration of most schemes within a range of services provided by the parent organisations meant that schemes' annual incomes were often difficult to establish. This was most especially the case with the local authority schemes, very few of which gave any estimated annual income figures. The only reliable data collected, therefore, relate to the schemes being run wholly or partly by the voluntary sector (including housing associations). For this reason, and because the funding issues relating to the two types of parent organisation differ, each will be discussed separately.

Local authority schemes

All 48 local authority schemes were being funded from within their respective housing department budgets. Scheme managers evidently found great difficulty in establishing the annual cost of these schemes, and none gave estimates of scheme income. Establishing staff costs was the main problem with assessing income, since scheme work could be the responsibility of more than one housing officer, who may be completing the work as only part of their job description. For example, one of the project managers who was interviewed worked on a local authority rent deposit scheme, which took up only part of her time. Although the manager was responsible for the overall running of the scheme, other officers in the department were, as part of their job description, responsible for recovering the loan from the clients and assessing client suitability for the scheme.

Although no data on the actual cost of the local authority schemes were available, it is still possible to draw important conclusions about their funding. Unlike funding for the voluntary sector schemes (as will be seen in the next section), there was a high degree of confidence that the local authority schemes would continue to be funded in the long term. Data from the questionnaire returns showed that 77 per cent of local authority schemes considered that securing long-term funding was not a problem at all. Both the local authority scheme managers who were interviewed thought that their councils would continue to offer help with access, and did not foresee any withdrawal of commitment.

Table 2.2
Voluntary sector scheme annual incomes (1993/4)

	number
£0-10,000	12
£10,001-20,000	19
£20,001-30,000	16
£30,001-40,000	5
£40,001-50,000	6
£50,001-60,000	5
£60,001+	4
Total	67
Source: postal survey	

Voluntary sector schemes

More information on funding was available with respect to the voluntary sector schemes. This did not mean that the schemes were any less intensively integrated into the work of the parent organisation: there was still a heavy degree of input into access work from other staff members including administrators, line managers, secretarial staff and fundraisers. For the purposes of funding applications, however, it was perhaps more likely that the scheme had a designated worker spending all their time on access work which meant that costs were more easily discernible. Data on annual income were available for over 60 cases. As Table 2.2 shows, the majority of schemes - 47 (70 per cent) - had an income of £30,000 or less a year.

Revenue funding came from a variety of sources, with some schemes relying on a complex patchwork of grants and donations, as Table 2.3 demonstrates.

Table 2.3
Numbers of voluntary sector schemes receiving proportions of funding from a range of sources in 1993/4

| Source of funding | Numbers receiving a proportion of funding | | | |
| | Proportions of funding | | | |
	0%	1-50%	51-99%	100%
Churches	55	10	2	1
Charitable trusts	47	17	2	2
Department of the Environment	12	15	19	22
Local authorities	55	12	1	0
Local businesses	64	4	0	0
Local charities	60	8	0	0
Private donations	52	16	0	0
Social services	61	6	1	0
(Total 68 schemes)				
Source: postal survey				

There was heavy reliance on funding from the s73 programme, with 22 of the schemes receiving 100 per cent funding from this source, and a further 19 receiving most of their funding in this way. Reliance on charitable giving was also extensive. Forty schemes received money from local churches, charities or charitable trusts and a further 16 had income from private donations, although only six schemes had any of these as their main source of funding. Income from statutory authorities (aside from the Department of the Environment) was limited. Only 13 schemes had funding from their local authority, and seven had income from the social services. The least likely source of income, however, was local businesses, which only contributed a small percentage of funding to four of the schemes.

The overriding characteristic of voluntary sector funding was its precarious nature. It seemed to be the case that start-up funds for new schemes were fairly easy to secure, but that long-term revenue funding was difficult to find. Many of the schemes were in receipt of s73 funding, for example, but this grant is given for a limited time period, and is tapered so that in its final year it contributes only 50 per cent to a scheme's income. The s73 programme's expectation is that continued funding for schemes will come from sources including local businesses, but as one manager commented, *'the government seems to think this is going to happen. I see no evidence of it'*. Charitable trusts also seemed willing to make initial grants, but tended not to make long-term commitments, according to one project worker:

> *Some of the big charities like Crisis, Children in Need, said initially they didn't mind starting you off - starting off a new project. But now they're looking to fund other new projects and what they're saying is, 'Well, if you're so vital to the local scene, the local authority should be funding you'. But unfortunately the local authority might think, yes we're very vital, but they haven't got any money because they're hitting budgets and having cuts and so there's no funding from them either.*
>
> (Project worker, Northwest Scheme)

After the initial set-up grant, alternative forms of income have to be sought, and in many cases applications are made to charity sources. Managers were generally unhappy about their reliance on this form of funding, which was considered to be only a short-term solution: *'if we go to another charity you've only got the problem delayed for another year'*. Data from the questionnaires show that this dilemma was common: 83 per cent of voluntary sector schemes considered securing long-term funding to be frequently or constantly a problem.

When asked about their long-term plans, the project managers revealed three strategies, each of which they saw as carrying some disadvantages. The first strategy was to continue applications for individual grants from charitable trusts, donations and statutory authorities. This approach was seen to be workable in the short term, but did not give any degree of security in the long term. At least one of the project managers interviewed said that the scheme had applied for funding from every possible source in the last few years, and their options were running out. A second approach was to modify the nature of the scheme to ensure that funding could be more formally secured from a statutory authority. The County Scheme, for example, was considering shifting its emphasis to finding supported lodgings for people with special needs, and entering into a service agreement with the local social services department. The third approach was to try and induce the local authority to take over the project entirely. This sort of take-over of the scheme was envisaged by one of the parent organisations, which would then be free to develop other work. All these options anticipated the possibility of either a scheme coming to the end of its funding, or the nature of its work changing to ensure continuity.

Deposit guarantee funds

Seventy-three schemes (45 per cent) gave guarantees in the place of paying cash to landlords, to cover deposits. Table 2.4 indicates the levels of funding reserved to cover the issue of guarantees.

Table 2.4
Funds reserved to cover the issue of guarantees

Cash in fund	proportion of schemes
	%
£-5000	39
£5001-10,000	24
£10,001-20,000	21
£20,001-30,000	13
£30,001+	3
	100
(Base = 62)	
Source: postal survey	

Sixty-three per cent of schemes had bond funds of £10,000 or less. Two schemes had bond funds in excess of £45,000, but these were atypical. With the exception of these outliers, the average total of guarantee fund was £11,163.

Schemes were asked from which sources they had received grants for the guarantee fund. Table 2.5 gives information on the proportions of schemes receiving funding from a range of sources.

Table 2.5 shows that, overall, local authorities were the most common source: 58 per cent of schemes had received some money from local authorities for their guarantee fund. Taking local authority schemes and voluntary sector schemes separately, however, a different picture emerged. Eighty-nine per cent of local authority guarantee funds had received funding internally from other parts of the local authority. None of the voluntary sector schemes were able to self-finance themselves in this manner. Instead, they were much more reliant on churches, charitable trusts, and private donations. A handful of schemes noted other sources of funding. For example, one scheme had been given a grant by the local parish council, and three of the schemes had received money for their guarantee fund from the Welsh Office as part of the s73 grant programme. This sort of grant for guarantee funds is not available in England.

Table 2.5
Proportions of schemes receiving funding for their guarantee fund from a range of sources

Source	All schemes %	Local authority Schemes %	Voluntary Sector Schemes %
Churches	29	4	44
Charitable trusts	27	0	44
Local authorities	58	89	39
Businesses	10	0	15
Private donations	29	4	44
Social services	10	0	15
(Base = 161)			
Note - more than one source of funding could be specified			
Source: postal survey			

Six of the case study schemes issued guarantees. In all cases these were voluntary sector schemes, which had built up guarantee funds through one-off grants and donations. None of the scheme managers showed any degree of certainty that their guarantee fund could be topped up to accommodate payments out to compensate landlords. The only scheme which had thought through a long-term strategy was the Southwest Scheme. The manager of the Scheme had estimated that they were losing approximately £2,000 a year, and had started up a system whereby individual donors agreed to pledge payments of £100 should a guarantee be called on.

Conclusion

The growth of help with access problems has been a relatively recent phenomenon. Schemes have mostly been developed by organisations already operating in the area of housing need. Access schemes were often an additional service developed after recognition of the need for help with getting into private renting: for example, a common scenario was the establishment of an access scheme to counter move-on difficulties experienced by hostel residents. Funding for local authority schemes was seen to be much more secure in the long term, compared with funding for voluntary sector schemes. With these sorts of schemes, income had often only been secured in the short term, and the possibility of schemes being operated as they stood in the long term was called into question by the limited availability of revenue funding. A similar pattern was repeated with respect to funding to back the issue of guarantees to cover deposits. The majority of local authority schemes had funds which had been financed internally. Voluntary sector schemes had been more reliant on one-off payments. There seemed little evidence amongst the voluntary sector schemes of strategies to deal with the erosion of their guarantee funds.

Chapter Three
Dealing with Clients

Introduction

This chapter looks at issues relating to schemes' management of clients, including the numbers of clients helped; restrictions in types of clients taken on; and referral arrangements. The chapter shows that there were marked differences in approach between local authority-run schemes and those managed by voluntary sector agencies.

Numbers of clients

In terms of the number of clients helped, there was considerable diversity in the size of the schemes. The postal survey returns showed that five schemes each dealt with over five hundred clients in the year 1993/4, two of which had helped over a thousand people each. These five schemes were very much an exception, however. With these schemes excluded, the average number of clients helped in 1993/4 was 92, as Table 3.1 shows. There were differences in the average number of clients helped by schemes of different status. Local authorities took, on average, 60 clients. Voluntary sector agencies, however, helped an average of 104 clients. There was also a difference between client numbers according to whether schemes were giving help with the payment of deposits. Schemes which gave help - either through giving cash or issuing guarantees - took, on average, 74 clients in 1993/4. Schemes which gave no help with deposits were more likely to be helping larger numbers, and were taking an average of 117 clients.

To explain why there was such diversity between the numbers of clients helped requires reference to a number of factors. The schemes helping very large numbers of clients (500+) included offering help through the wide circulation of a vacancies list. Local authorities were helping smaller numbers of clients, and this was possibly because they tended to apply more rigorous restrictions on the type of client helped, as will be seen later in this chapter. Deposit-help schemes assisted fewer clients than schemes giving no help with deposits, perhaps because of constraints imposed by the finite nature of a deposit fund. It should also be stressed that schemes might apply different criteria when counting clients: some, for example, might include all those clients who had received advice, however brief such a consultation might be, and others might only count clients who had been issued with guarantees.

Table 3.1

Average number of clients helped in 1993/4, by scheme status and scheme type

	average number of clients helped	(base)
All	92	(86)
Local authority	60	(22)
Voluntary sector	104	(64)
Help with deposits	74	(47)
No help with deposits	117	(35)
Source: postal survey		

The case study managers were asked whether their scheme was able to meet all the demand for their particular service. In all cases except one the manager said that they could cope with current demand, and had not had to institute any system of prioritisation. The exception was the London Scheme, but this scheme had a well-defined population (families in temporary accommodation) which it had been set up to reduce. Generally, schemes indicated that they were able to assess all the clients coming through to the scheme, but that certain circumstances would limit throughputs. Two constraining factors were highlighted. Two of the schemes said that limited supply of suitable properties was creating bottlenecks in building up numbers of clients eligible for help but for whom no accommodation could be found. The Westerbury Scheme, for example, estimated that only around one sixth of its clients who had an initial assessment then went on to secure accommodation. The reason for this low throughput was because suitable properties were in limited supply in their area. A further constraint on providing help was related to funds for access costs. In cases where funds were limited, only a finite number of clients could be helped. One of the scheme managers said that they had to turn people away at times when their deposit fund was low. Another manager commented that their fund of £5000 could help few people with deposit payments, since in their area it was common for landlords to ask for sums of up to £500.

Restrictions

The majority of schemes (86 per cent) operated one or more restrictions which defined the type of client they intended to help. The most common restrictions applied amongst all schemes were: only taking people from the local area (37 per cent); only taking people who were in receipt of low income (32 per cent); only taking people who would be eligible for housing benefit (24 per cent); and only taking clients who were capable of independent living (30 per cent). Other restrictions, however, were more specific to a particular type of parent organisation. Voluntary sector schemes were much more likely to include amongst their restrictions: only taking people who were under 25; only taking people who were non-statutory homeless; and only taking people who were single. By contrast, local authorities most often applied restrictions which included only taking people who were statutory homeless; only taking applications from families; and only helping people on the council's housing waiting list. Table 3.2 gives the proportions by scheme status.

Table 3.2
Client restrictions by scheme status

Scheme status	All	Local Authority	Voluntary Sector
	%	%	%
From local area	37	38	6
Low income	32	31	32
Independent living	30	27	32
Housing benefit	24	25	23
Single	32	13	41
Non-statutory homeless	26	10	33
Young people (under 25)	24	2	34
Statutory homeless	14	40	3
Waiting list	8	19	3
Families	4	10	2
No restrictions	14	13	14
(Base)	(159)	(46)	(113)
Note - columns do not total 100 because more than one restriction could be applied			
Source: postal survey			

The case study managers discussed the rationale behind the restrictions they imposed. Restrictions relating to the economic status of the client (in receipt of low income and on housing benefit) were evidently there to ensure that help would be targeted at those in most need. Reasons behind the decision to help only those capable of independent living were more complex and included limitations in staff time, compounded by the belief that other agencies were there to deal with clients with severe need: 'the people who have serious social, mental problems ought to be the responsibility of the social services'. Schemes should therefore target their help at those clients ineligible for statutory assistance. A further reason not to deal with people with support needs was the fact that finding such people accommodation in the private rented sector was simply not a suitable course of action: 'our landlords aren't actually carers, our landlords are landlords'.

It was more commonly the case, though, that schemes mentioned the need to keep landlords happy by sending them tenants likely to be able to sustain a tenancy without difficulty:

> *Because if we didn't, we would not get landlords. We might get one landlord take one person but, if that's a disaster, a lot of other landlords are going to know about it in no time at all and it's really for the benefit of the clients who are not in these states, that we felt that* [it was necessary to introduce these restrictions]. *If you have a couple of disasters, you just wreck the whole system.*
> (Project manager, Southwest Scheme)

Another scheme, which did deal with younger clients needing often intensive support, said that they had difficulty keeping landlords:

> *Sometimes a landlord can be really sympathetic to start with and then very quickly after they've lost their third telly or whatever, can be very quickly not very sympathetic at all.*
> (Project worker, Northwest Scheme)

For project managers, the failure of a tenancy because of the client's bad behaviour, meant that 'we may lose a property in future which somebody else could make good use of'. Also, such failures might run down deposit funds - through payments out for damage or rent in lieu of notice - which meant that help would be available to less people. Dealing only with clients capable of independent living, therefore, was usually seen less as a support issue, and more as a way of helping more people by protecting the deposit fund and ensuring continued good relations with local landlords.

The schemes operating restrictions which included clients having to be young, to be non-statutorily homeless, and to be single were often working in a context where these characteristics applied to the clients helped by the parent organisation. For example, the Westerbury Scheme, as has been seen, had been set up to help move young people out of the parent organisation's hostel. Furthermore, the single non-statutory homeless is a group targeted for assistance by the s73 grant programme and, as Chapter two demonstrated, many schemes were receiving s73 funding. Some schemes refused to help statutory homeless people because it was considered that if it was at all possible that a client may get a council tenancy, then they should be encouraged to apply.

As has been seen, local authorities often restricted their help using criteria which included taking only families, taking only statutory homeless people, and taking only those on the council waiting list. It was evident that in these cases the access scheme was operating as part of the local authority's responsibility to help certain types of people in housing need. The way in which the access scheme contributed towards discharging this responsibility varied. Some local authorities were offering help with getting into private rented properties to households who were statutory homeless but not in priority need. In other cases, however, the help was given as a discharge of duty to house. The manager of the London Scheme was running a scheme which restricted its help to dealing only with statutorily homeless families which were in temporary accommodation, and on the council waiting list. The tenancies created were intended to last at least 12 months. Although the clients were guaranteed the offer of a council house at the end of that period, the manager did express the hope that some of the families might choose to stay in the private rented sector. Some of the local authorities which were operating schemes only helping families on the waiting list commented that the schemes had tended not to be particularly successful, and that take up was limited. It was thought that the families preferred to wait for council accommodation rather than be housed in the private rented sector. This factor is another possible explanation of the fact that local authority schemes tended to have a smaller number of clients.

A small number of schemes (14 per cent) had no restrictions at all in the types of client they helped. In some cases, this was a reflection of the way in which the scheme operated. For example, the Metropolitan Scheme had no restrictions since its list of vacancies was available to anyone choosing to come to the shop-front office.

The case study managers gave information about the way in which restrictions operated in practice. The local authority schemes, because they tended to be more formalised, did not foresee any situations in which they would take clients who did not fit the restrictions criteria. The voluntary sector agencies, on the other hand, were more likely to be flexible on such issues as taking people who were outside their usual specified age group or people who were in work, for example. One scheme said that in practice, despite the restrictions, it did not turn anyone away providing they looked like they might be able to sustain a tenancy. Alternatively, those schemes which in principle operated a fairly open policy did sometimes restrict their services in practice, by refusing to continue dealing with clients who had been violent to staff members or who had a history of wrecking properties.

Referrals

The postal questionnaire collected information on the routes by which schemes usually took on clients. The majority of schemes (82 per cent) drew their clients from a variety of sources, with very few relying on a single source. The most popular route by which clients were taken on was self referral: 21 per cent of schemes took on more than half of their clients this way. On average, schemes took 37 per cent of their clients through self referral; 25 per cent were referred from other parts of the parent organisation; 15 per cent were referred from voluntary agencies; and 24 per cent were referred from statutory agencies. There were some exceptions. One third of local authority schemes took all their clients as internal referrals from other parts of the housing department.

This pattern of referrals was also reflected in the interviews with clients, who were asked about the way in which they had first got in touch with the scheme. Fourteen of the 39 clients were self-referrals. In one case - the Metropolitan Scheme - the clients had approached the scheme because of its shop-front offices. In most other cases, the clients had found out about the scheme through word of mouth - often through people who had been helped themselves. Some of the clients heard through letting agents or landlords who had either used the scheme to find tenants or who had had tenants who used the scheme. The second most common way that the clients came into contact with schemes was through being referred by a worker at the hostel in which they were staying. In all these cases, the client had approached the hostel worker and said that they had wanted to move out, and the hostel worker had said that the scheme would help. By contrast, all the clients of the London Scheme had been contacted themselves by the scheme manager, as being suitable for transferring from temporary accommodation to a property in the private rented sector.

Scheme managers were asked also about the process of referrals. Three of the schemes took referrals from a single source only. Two of these schemes were the local authority-run schemes, both of which only took referrals from the homelessness sections of the housing department. One voluntary sector scheme - the Churches Scheme - also only took referrals from the council housing department, a procedure which reflected the fact that the scheme was run entirely by volunteers with no parent organisation, and was reliant on the council to undertake a client vetting procedure.

In all the remaining case study schemes, referrals were taken from a range of sources, including the council's housing advice centre, the social services, the local YMCA, the CAB and the probation service. In some cases, the system was formalised. The Southwest Scheme, for example, took up to 25 families a year from the council's housing department, for which a set fee was paid. These sorts of arrangements tended to be exceptional, since most schemes' referral procedures were quite open and informal.

For the most part, the referral systems worked well and schemes were happy with the appropriateness of the clients who were being sent through. The most frequently iterated complaint was with the social services department, which some schemes thought often sent clients who were not capable of living independently. The Southwest Scheme, for example, had lost money on all the social services clients it had dealt with, because the department had not made sure that the clients were able to live without support, and in all cases, the tenancies had broken down with money owing to the landlord. As a consequence, the scheme was trying to arrange for the department to back guarantees issued on its nominated clients.

Conclusion

Examining the way in which clients were dealt with has further contributed to the process of characterising schemes by type and by status. It was more likely that written guarantee schemes dealt with smaller numbers of clients than schemes which were not issuing written guarantees. It was also more likely that local authority schemes dealt with smaller numbers of clients than the voluntary sector schemes. This finding is probably tied to the fact that local authority schemes were often more restrictive in the types of client they helped, and tended to only deal with families, with people who were statutory homeless, and with people on the council waiting list. Taking all schemes together, most took their clients from a range of sources, although self-referral was the most common route by which clients were taken on. The interviews with clients showed that they had usually found out about the scheme through word of mouth.

Chapter Four
Dealing with Landlords

Introduction

This chapter will discuss the nature of the working relationship between schemes and landlords. The majority of the schemes were actively involved in gathering information on the rental market in their area, usually through the compilation of lists of landlords and details of their properties. It was clear that the nature of the private rental market in which schemes worked frequently constrained their ability to secure accommodation for their clients. Schemes were responding to these constraints, however, by implementing strategies to increase the amount of stock available.

Despite the often limited availability of accommodation, many schemes imposed restrictions on the landlords they dealt with. For example, landlords would only be used if they charged rents at or below average market levels and offered good quality accommodation meeting health and safety requirements. The chapter will show how the imposition of restrictions differed according to scheme status and type, and will also discuss the way in which restrictions were imposed in practice. The final part of the chapter will look at the types of accommodation which were secured for clients.

The rental market

The great majority of the schemes collected information on the private rented sector in their area. In most cases, the information collected related to landlords and their properties. Details were stored by landlord name in files or index cards, with notes which included the nature of the properties let by the landlord, the rents charged, and whether advance payments were required. Notes were also usually kept about any visits to the property made by the scheme. The London Scheme kept perhaps the most extensive landlord records, which also included whether or not there had been a rent officer determination on the property, and its the tenancy history. Other schemes kept little more than a list of landlord names and contact numbers. Differences in approach reflected to some degree the number of landlords a particular scheme was dealing with. The London

Scheme had on its register over 500 landlords. Some of the smaller schemes were dealing with less than 10 landlords at any one time, and the worker usually had a familiarity with the landlords and their properties which meant that the formalised listing of information was not necessary.

Ways in which the information was collected varied. The Westerbury Scheme was, at the time of the interview with its manager, about to undertake a large-scale survey of all the landlords in its area. In the majority of cases, however, information was gathered on a less formal basis by using newspaper advertisements and through word of mouth from clients and other agencies working in the same area. In some cases, the scheme actively encouraged approaches from landlords. The City Scheme, for example, often advertised for properties on the local radio. Landlords contacting the scheme were sent a form which asked for details of property type, rent charged and advance payments required.

It was clear that gathering this sort of information was a very necessary activity in contributing to schemes' understandings of the peculiarities of the particular rental market in which they were operating, and that schemes adapted to some degree to meet the market requirements. The most obvious example of this was landlords asking for advance payments, which tended to vary from area to area: for example, in one of the case study schemes, landlords almost never required a deposit, but always wanted rent in advance; and in another area it was clear that rent in advance and deposit had become merged together. This was because it was quite easy to get rent in advance payments from the social fund, and landlords were calling these payments 'rent in advance', but accepting them as deposits since the tenant was given the payment back at the end of the tenancy.

For the most part, the schemes were gathering information in the context of a rental market which constrained their attempts to secure accommodation for their clients. The supply of accommodation was the main difficulty. The postal survey data showed that 69 per cent of schemes considered that the limited availability of reasonable-quality accommodation was constantly or frequently a problem. There were a number of schemes which reported acute difficulty, and in all these cases the problem was a consequence of there being competition from other tenant types. Schemes located in tourist towns had particular problems, since rents could be high and landlords were geared up to dealing with seasonal trade. Also, schemes in towns close to military bases said that landlords were more willing to let to military families.

As with funding and client selection, there was also a contrast between voluntary sector and local authority schemes in their experience of the problem of limited accommodation. Voluntary sector schemes were much more likely to find the limited availability of accommodation a difficulty: 85 per cent of such schemes reported this to be constantly or frequently a problem. In comparison, only one third of local authorities did not consider limited accommodation a problem, or had experienced it only occasionally. The contrasting experience of schemes of different status suggests that the actual supply of accommodation was in some areas less a problem than schemes' ability to gain access to it.

These findings suggest that it is inadvisable to make generalisations about the working relationship between schemes and landlords. Interviews with project managers confirm this view. It became evident that voluntary sector and local authority schemes could have a varied experience of the range of subsectors in the rental market. Amongst the case study schemes, three particular types of relationship were evident: the relationship between voluntary sector schemes and the bottom end of the private rented sector; the relationship between the voluntary sector schemes and landlords further up the rental market; and the relationship between local authority schemes and 'reluctant' or sideline landlords.

Many of the voluntary sector scheme managers commented that they had very little difficulty in finding properties at the very bottom end of the private rented sector of the market - in bed and breakfast hotels, bedsits and rooms in houses in multiple occupation (HMOs). These properties were owned by landlords with extended experience of taking people on housing benefit, who were willing to let to people without advance payments. The County Scheme in particular relied on landlords at the very bottom end of the market, since it was often placing clients who had had alcohol dependency problems and who would have been difficult to place elsewhere. Landlords using this scheme saw it as an easy way of getting a reasonable supply of tenants. Many schemes commented that although properties at the bottom end of the market were more easily available, they did not like to use it because of its poor quality, and because clients were unlikely to stay in that property type for any length of time.

In contrast, there was a less equitable relationship between voluntary sector schemes and business landlords further up the rental market. These landlords were more likely to be letting self-contained flats or houses, but were unwilling to let to people on housing benefit or to let a property without advance payments of both rent and deposits. The Charity Scheme had managed to develop a relationship with this type of landlord. However, the relationship entailed a greater degree of input from the scheme in offering deposit guarantees and payments of rent until the housing benefit claim was sorted out. The Charity Scheme landlords viewed their local scheme in a way altogether differently from the landlords of the County Scheme. The latter saw their local scheme as a useful provider of tenants. The Charity Scheme landlords, on the other hand, considered that they had a plentiful supply of working tenants for their properties. If they took on a scheme tenant, it was as 'a favour' which entailed considerable persuasion.

A different relationship again was evident between a local authority scheme and 'reluctant' or sideline landlords, who tended to have only one or two properties which had perhaps at one time been family homes but were now unused or were waiting to be sold once the owner-occupied property market picked up (Bevan *et al.*, 1995). The London Scheme had found a plentiful supply of this sort of landlord, who were usually offering two or three bedroomed houses or larger. The success experienced by the scheme in gaining access to such a good supply of properties probably rested with the scheme being run by the council which inspired in the landlord a feeling of confidence. This need for security was especially the case for relatively inexperienced landlords, who might see becoming involved in a council-run scheme as a fairly stable way of dealing with letting. London Scheme landlords often made no distinctions between the placement work done by the scheme, and the payment of housing benefit. It was all done by 'the Council' who, it was believed, had taken over the whole tenancy. One landlord, for example, praised the scheme: *'I don't feel I have to concern myself about the financial state, or worry about it. Somebody else will have to do that'*. The three different experiences described here demonstrate that generalising about schemes' relationship with landlords is inadvisable. Schemes could find some sectors of the rental market more difficult to engage with than others, depending on the services which were offered.

Although it is unwise to generalise about the relationships between schemes and landlords, it was certainly the case that the great majority of schemes (90 per cent) spent some time trying to increase the amount of stock available to their clients. Some schemes had become involved in the development of new properties. For example, the Westerbury Scheme had made close contact with a builder working in the area, and had persuaded him to renovate property which would then be let to scheme clients. In some cases, schemes were being successful in generating lettings from property owners who had not let before. As might be expected, however, this was more often the case with local authority schemes than with the voluntary sector agencies.

For the most part, schemes tried to generate more accommodation by trying to persuade landlords in the better-quality, self-contained property market to let to scheme tenants. This strategy had been successful with some of the landlords interviewed, who said that they would not normally have let to people who were unemployed or in receipt of housing benefit, but were persuaded to do so by the scheme. This was particularly the case for the Charity Scheme. The Scheme expected the clients to locate properties, for which it would provide a deposit guarantee and payment of rent until the housing benefit cheque came through. The Scheme dealt with a lot of property management agents who said that normally they would not let to this type of client, but had done so because of the financial guarantees being offered.

Almost all the scheme managers interviewed said that they thought that their scheme offered good inducements to landlords, including smoothing out any difficulties with housing benefit applications and finding tenants without charging a fee. The one exception was the Townshire Scheme, which considered that its scheme was quite unpopular with the property agents it worked through. Indeed, many property managers had increased the deposits required to a level beyond the limit usually paid out by the scheme.

Landlord restrictions

Although most schemes found the limited availability of suitable accommodation a problem, few schemes (seven per cent) applied no restrictions at all on the landlords they dealt with. The postal survey asked whether the following criteria were always applied: charging rents at or below the average market level for the area; providing good quality accommodation meeting health and safety requirements; and providing a rent book with a full rent breakdown. In addition the survey was asked whether landlords were to provide a minimum six-month tenancy. Although this is an enforceable legislative minimum requirement for tenancy agreements, it was possible for some schemes to use only lodgings arrangements, or hotels and hostels where licensing agreements applied. Table 4.1 gives the proportion of schemes (by status and type) applying each restriction.

Table 4.1
Landlord restrictions always applied, by scheme status and scheme type

	All %	Local Authority %	Voluntary Sector %	Deposit help %	Non-deposit help %
No convictions for harassment/ illegal eviction	73	78	70	72	74
Charge no more than average market rent	71	79	68	77	62
Good quality accommodation	62	74	57	67	53
Six-month tenancies	56	79	46	62	45
Providing rent book	45	55	40	46	42
(Base)	(147)	(43)	(103)	(88)	(51)
Note - more than one restriction could be applied					
Source: postal survey					

As Table 4.1 shows, the most frequently applied criterion, taking all schemes together, was the requirement that landlords should not have convictions for harassment or illegal eviction (applied by 73 per cent of schemes). Also applied by nearly three quarters of schemes was the requirement for landlords to charge no more than average market rent (applied by 71 per cent of schemes) - a reflection of the need to ensure that all the eligible rent charged would be covered by housing benefit. The third most popular requirement was that landlords should provide a minimum six-month tenancy. That landlords were required to provide good quality accommodation, and were to provide a rent book - indicators of good management practice - were slightly less usually applied, at 62 per cent and 45 per cent of schemes respectively. Table 4.1 also shows that the imposition of restrictions differed according to scheme status. Voluntary sector schemes were less likely to apply particular restrictions than local authority schemes, particularly in respect to landlords being required to create minimum six-month tenancies: 46 per cent of voluntary sector schemes had this requirement, compared with 79 per cent of local authority schemes.

A more telling difference, however, depended on whether or not schemes gave financial help with deposits. Schemes offering a guarantee or cash help were much more likely to apply restrictive criteria than those schemes not offering this sort of help. Thus, for example, 77 per cent of schemes giving financial help with deposits always or sometimes used landlords who were charging a market rent, compared with 62 per cent of schemes not helping with deposits. Sixty-seven per cent of schemes helping with deposits always used landlords offering good quality accommodation, whilst only 53 per cent of non-financial deposit help schemes did so; and 62 per cent of deposit-help schemes always used landlords offering a minimum six-month tenancy compared with 45 per cent of non-financial deposit help schemes. The comparative differences indicate that schemes giving financial help with deposits were more likely to offer better-quality accommodation to their clients, and use landlords with better management practices. Schemes offering no financial help with deposits were in a weaker position, comparatively, in being less likely to be able to impose restrictions.

Discussion with the project managers explored how restrictions were applied in practice. In two cases, restrictions were be applied at a 'pre-register' stage: to be involved with the scheme, landlords had to fit a given set of criteria. This was most noticeably the case with the London Borough Placement Scheme where, in order to be accepted by the scheme, landlords had to agree to a given rent level, to waive deposits, and to have no choice of tenant. This sort of process reflected a more formalised system of having an accommodation register which only included landlords 'approved' by the scheme.

For schemes not running formalised landlord-based registers, restrictions were applied differently. In instances where the scheme might expect the client to find the accommodation or where the scheme helped the client to look, restrictions became to some extent negotiable depending on the client wanting to be housed, and depending on the property. From the point of view of scheme managers, it was most often the case that restrictions on taking only good quality accommodation were not applied, since clients, often in desperate housing need, might be willing to take on a property despite poor conditions. One manager described a typical situation, where a meeting would take place between the tenant, the scheme manager and the landlord at the property for the first time:

> *I'm probably there to sign up, and at that stage the tenant is not interested in how many units of electricity they get for 50p, they just want to be in. So it's quite difficult to impose them* [restrictions]. *And also because it's not always easy to find accommodation for people. If* [the landlord's] *got a good standard of accommodation, but there's one or two things that you're not entirely happy with, and the tenant's going 'Yeah, yeah, yeah, when can I move in?', it's quite difficult.*
>
> (Project manager, Northern Scheme)

Thus the scheme might have restrictions which the client's particular preferences make difficult to apply. This way of working reflects the fact that 15 per cent of schemes were only sometimes able to apply restrictions on market rent; 14 per cent of schemes only sometimes imposed restrictions on good quality accommodation being provided; 26 per cent of schemes sometimes required landlords to offer a minimum six-month tenancy; and 30 per cent of schemes sometimes required the landlord to provide a rent book.

As was indicated at the beginning of this section, a small proportion of schemes (seven per cent) operated no restrictions at all. The postal survey showed that these schemes were most likely to be those offering no help with deposits, and so having little bargaining power with landlords. The Northwest Scheme, for example, said that it could not be fussy about landlords used because they were often agreeing to take on disruptive clients with no cash bonds or rent in advance. However, even schemes offering cash help with access costs might be forced to operate without applying criteria, if they were working in an area where supply of accommodation might be limited. The Churches Scheme, operating in a small tourist town with very high rents, said that they were '*so desperate for landlords that we haven't been very choosy*'.

Schemes were also asked whether their general restrictions were ordered in such a way as to provide lists of 'bad' or 'approved' landlords. Taking all schemes together, 36 per cent of schemes kept a list of bad landlords, with whom they would not deal. Two of the case study schemes had a bad landlord list, and in both cases there was some reliance on information from the housing advice centre. The Northern Scheme used a list from its local housing advice centre, with landlords highlighted as either 'not recommended' or simply 'do not use'. The 'not recommended' landlords were those with a history of complaints, but where there had been no incidents recorded in the last two years. The advice centre list was supplemented by the scheme with landlords they had come across and would not use, including landlords offering poor standards of accommodation and those charging too much for gas and electricity in properties where the landlord had fitted a meter. The London Scheme also used a bad landlord list, which included landlords who had a history of sustained harassment of, or violence against, tenants. In cases where the complaints were unsubstantiated, the scheme checked the landlord out itself.

Forty-six per cent of schemes had some sort of 'approved' landlord list. The concept of 'approved landlords' was discussed with the case study schemes. There was general agreement that approval should not simply imply that the landlord did not have a history of bad practice. Instead, good landlords were considered to be ones who responded on repairs, gave notice before they visited a property, and who stuck to the terms of the tenancy agreement. The Northwest Scheme judged its good landlords by the length of time tenants tended to stay in their properties.

Some scheme managers said that they had some reservations about the concepts of 'good' and 'approved' landlords. For some managers there were legal issues attached to actually putting together a list of bad landlords, and there was a sensitivity to possible libel action. These schemes said that they were often aware of which landlords to avoid in their area, and did not need to collate the information formally. On the question of approving landlords, there was some concern that approving a landlord implied a degree of recommendation to the client, perhaps creating a misunderstanding of a scheme's responsibility for the success of a tenancy. This is an issue which will be pursued in Chapter five.

Types of accommodation used

The postal survey asked schemes what proportion of their clients were placed into each of the following property types: self-contained flats or houses; HMOs; bedsits; lodgings; and temporary accommodation, including hostels and bed and breakfast hotels. Table 4.2 gives details of the average proportion of clients placed by different types of scheme in each sort of housing.

Table 4.2
Average proportion of clients placed in each accommodation type, by scheme status and scheme type

	All	Local Authority	Voluntary Sector	No help with deposits	Help with deposits
Self-contained flats/houses	47	78	34	35	60
Bedsits	19	9	23	22	17
Temporary accommodation	3	0	4	5	2
HMOs	19	9	23	25	13
Lodgings	11	3	15	13	8
Total	99	99	99	100	100
(Base)	(92)	(26)	(66)	(41)	(45)
NB - totals do not add up to 100 due to rounding					
Source: postal survey					

Taking all schemes together, on average nearly half of clients (47 per cent) were found self-contained accommodation. Placements in bedsits and HMOs each accounted for 19 per cent of clients, and lodgings a further 11 per cent. Temporary accommodation was used for only three per cent of clients.

Again, however, there were considerable differences according to the status of the scheme. Local authority schemes placed, on average, 78 per cent of their clients in self-contained accommodation, compared with voluntary sector schemes, which placed 34 per cent of their clients in that accommodation type. More than twice the number of voluntary sectors clients were placed in HMOs and bedsits than local authority scheme clients (46 per cent compared with 18 per cent). Local authorities made no use at all of temporary accommodation, but four per cent of voluntary sector schemes clients were placed in temporary housing.

Differences were similarly marked between schemes which did and did not offer financial help with deposits. Schemes giving financial help with deposits on average placed 60 per cent of their clients in self-contained accommodation, but only 35 per cent of clients of schemes not giving this help were secured self-contained housing. Schemes not giving financial help with deposits were also more heavily reliant on bedsits and HMOs - where advance payments were less likely to be required - placing 47 per cent of their clients in this accommodation type. Only 30 per cent of clients of financial deposit-help schemes were secured this type of housing.

These proportions underline the conclusion that local authority schemes and schemes offering financial help with deposits were in a stronger position in respect to dealing with landlords, in being able to secure more self-contained properties for their clients, and placing less reliance on shared accommodation. By contrast, voluntary sector schemes and schemes offering no financial help with deposits were much more heavily dependent on bedsits and HMOs.

Conclusion

The majority of schemes were actively compiling information about their local private rented sector, and the services they offered often reflected the peculiarities of that particular market. Most schemes were constrained to some degree by the nature of the housing market in the area where they were operating, especially if there was competition for rental properties from other groups. The relationship between schemes and landlords was found not to be uniform: depending on scheme type and status, and the sector of the rental market aimed at, landlords showed varying degrees of willingness to become involved in taking scheme tenants. Most schemes were making some attempt to try and increase the amount of property available to their clients, either by developing relationships with new landlords, or offering inducements to landlords to let to scheme clients.

Despite some difficulties with supply, almost all schemes operated some sort of restriction in deciding which landlords to deal with, and sometimes compiled lists of good and approved landlords. There was some variety in the way in which certain restrictions were operated. Local authority schemes and schemes offering help with deposits were more able to apply restrictive criteria than voluntary sector schemes or schemes offering no help with deposits. In some cases, being able to apply restrictions to landlords was compromised by the willingness of the client to take a property regardless of a scheme's recommendation. In looking at the types of accommodation used, the chapter shows that nearly half of all clients, on average, were placed in self-contained accommodation. Local authority schemes placed a larger proportion of their clients in self-contained housing. Bedsits and HMOs were more heavily used by voluntary sector schemes and schemes offering no help with deposits, each placing nearly half their clients in this sort of housing.

Section Two:

Services Schemes Offered

Chapter Five
Help Finding Somewhere to Live

Introduction

Most of the schemes in the postal survey (89 per cent) helped people to find somewhere to live. Although many of these schemes would have considered that they operated accommodation registers, this term creates confusion rather than giving a clear impression of the type of help given. The first section of this chapter offers alternative, and more exact, definitions. The chapter then goes on to explore in more detail how schemes helped people to find a place to live. The three essential elements of this task will be discussed: giving information on vacancies; matching tenant with landlord; and setting up a sustainable tenancy.

Defining accommodation registers

Before going on to discuss the ways in which people were helped into accommodation, it is necessary to clarify the terms used. The term 'accommodation register' implies a system of collecting landlord contacts and keeping details of their properties. Reference to the register might be made for appropriate vacancies once a client's housing preferences are known. In practice, schemes' activities in this area suggest that it would be more appropriate to define four types of register: registers of landlords and properties, collated to provide the scheme with information on the characteristics of the local private rented sector (landlord registers); registers of landlords who met certain restrictive criteria (approved landlord registers); lists of vacancies from landlords who may have been checked by the scheme (approved vacancy lists); and lists of vacancies not checked by the scheme (vacancy lists).

Chapter four has already shown that most schemes routinely collected information on the private rented sector in their area, and kept this information in the form of a landlord register. It was not always the case that schemes with landlord registers used the register to help people find somewhere to stay. Even with schemes which did help people find accommodation, the landlord register was not directly involved with the help given. None of the case study schemes which had landlord registers gave their clients access to these registers. Rather, the landlord register included material which the scheme used internally to inform its decisions on which services to offer, and which helped the scheme compare the accommodation it was securing for its clients with other properties in the local rental market.

Again, as Chapter four demonstrated, nearly half of all schemes kept a register of approved landlords. Landlords were only included in the register if they met certain criteria, including offering good quality accommodation, and having no convictions for harassment or illegal eviction. Schemes often visited landlords and vetted their property according to environmental health standards before they were placed on the register. In some cases, schemes with approved landlord lists only placed their clients in properties provided by these landlords. There was some resistance amongst case study schemes to the idea of having an approved landlord register, although they did actually manage these in practice. Caution was expressed about the legal implications of using the word 'approved'. As the Southwest Scheme manager commented, *'If you start approving a landlord, then you can become liable if they failed'*.

Some schemes ran approved vacancy lists. This could mean that vacancies were only included which came from landlords who were on the approved register; or simply that vacancies advertised by landlords known to be bad were omitted. Approved vacancy lists contained lists of currently available properties, and included a landlord's name, contact number, type of property, rent required, and whether a deposit or rent in advance were wanted. The list was usually freely available to clients, who could take it away and use it to find somewhere to stay. A small number of schemes ran vacancy lists which were not in any way vetted, but which reproduced all the information on properties available that appeared in the local press, so saving clients the cost of buying newspapers.

Schemes were unlikely to run all types of register or list, although almost all schemes were collating a landlord register, or were thinking of doing so. The value of this activity has been underlined in Chapter four. The most common combinations were to run a landlord register together with a vacancy list, and an approved landlord register alongside an approved vacancy list. Some schemes only collated a property register, and some schemes only operated a vacancy list.

There was often little or no rationale for schemes' decisions to take a particular approach. In the one case where a conscious decision had been made, the choice had rested on the limited nature of the landlord/vacancy information needing to be organised: according to the manager of the Southwest Scheme, *'There's no point in keeping a terrific register for something, there are never any more than half a dozen places vacant at any one time'*.

The general inability of the majority of schemes to be self-analytical on this point probably rested on the fact that little research has been completed on different approaches to accommodation register management, and managers evidently had not consciously taken any decisions to work one way in preference to any other. It was even the case that some managers did not think that they even ran a register or vacancy list, although it was clear that they did when asked in more detail about how they helped people find somewhere to stay.

Another factor explaining managers' inability to assess the rationale behind their approach to register and vacancy list management was the fact that, in practice, the registers and the lists were often kept in a fairly informal way, had developed haphazardly over time, and were in some instances quite limited in the number of landlords and vacancies covered. It was therefore understandable that schemes found classifying this sort of work difficult. For example, one scheme's 'vacancy list' was a pin board which had information on vacancies on slips of paper. The information came from landlords calling the scheme. The board rarely had more than around half a dozen bits of paper attached to it at any one time. In another case, an 'approved landlord register' was in reality a small box containing index cards holding the telephone numbers of what were considered good landlords. Because the scheme was working with only a small number of landlords - perhaps less than a dozen - it was unnecessary to keep more formal records. The scheme worker's information on the properties the landlords had was in the form of 'working knowledge'.

To summarise, although it is possible to define four different types of accommodation register - landlord registers, approved landlord registers, approved vacancy lists and vacancy lists - none of the scheme managers had made a conscious decision as to which approach to take, based on any assessment of the advantages and disadvantages of one approach over another. It is possible to conclude, however, that most of the schemes did not formally institute some process of landlord register management, because they were only dealing with a small number of landlords and vacancies.

Giving information on vacancies

There were two ways in which schemes helped people find available accommodation: keeping either type of vacancy list; and supporting the client through the search process, perhaps by offering the use of a phone, or contacting landlords on behalf of the client. Three of the scheme managers who were interviewed undertook both these activities. The City Scheme put together a list of vacancies compiled from landlords contacting the scheme. Vacancies offered by landlords known to be bad were not included. The list was circulated to various organisations. Landlords were expected to keep the scheme up to date on whether vacancies were filled, although the scheme called up landlords from time to time to check. Clients approaching the scheme for help in finding somewhere to live were given the list and access to a telephone. In some cases, if the client requested it, the scheme worker would help the client go through the list. A similar arrangement was made by the Northwest Scheme. This scheme kept information on vacancies from advertisements in the local paper and from other agencies working in the area (*'we swap landlords'*). The list was kept up to date by the scheme calling round or telephoning landlords. Clients were helped by the scheme worker going through the list of vacancies with them, to find something suitable. The scheme worker might also take the client to meet the landlord and view the property.

The Metropolitan Scheme was slightly different. This scheme produced a weekly list compiled from advertisements in the newspaper. The list was freely available to anyone coming to the Scheme's shop-front office. Some landlords did not bother to put their vacancies in the newspaper, and simply contacted the list directly. Unlike the other two schemes, there was no vetting, and all vacancies were included. Clients were given the list and access to a telephone, although the scheme would call the landlord if the client did not feel confident enough to do so.

Other schemes did not offer lists of vacancies, but gave their clients other help in looking. For example, the Westerbury Scheme did not formally set out to help people find somewhere to live: it expected clients to find places, for which the scheme would provide deposits. Although the Scheme did not proactively collate information on vacancies, landlords sometimes called when they had properties available. If a suitable vacancy came in at the same time as a client, then the scheme would pass the information to the client. For the most part however, when the client requested it, the scheme supported the client through the process of looking by providing newspapers, allowing the client the use of the phone, and sometimes taking the client to see properties. The Southwest Scheme operated in a similar way. Clients were given details of vacancies which landlords called in with, but were generally expected to follow up these vacancies themselves.

It is important to stress that there was a great variety in the degree of involvement in providing approved vacancies lists and supporting search activity. Even those schemes which did not set out to collect information on available accommodation often had one or two vacancies on hand, or might perhaps call round landlords on their register to ask if anything was currently vacant. It was also the case that schemes just producing lists of accommodation would not refuse to offer to help someone actually look for somewhere, even if this only included free access to the use of a telephone.

The degree of overlap between the two sorts of help does indicate, however, that each had advantages and disadvantages which schemes were willing to exploit or avoid. Some schemes perceived a psychological advantage to the client in only offering a vacancy list of whatever sort. The client would then be encouraged to make a choice themselves, and so not be caught up in some sort of dependency relationship with the scheme. The main disadvantage of keeping any sort of vacancy list was ensuring that the list was up to date, so the client would not waste time chasing properties which had already been let. Keeping lists up to date therefore became a necessary and sometimes time-consuming administrative task, unless the vacancies were only advertised for a limited time period, and then automatically removed, as was the case with the Metropolitan Scheme.

The alternative approach - supporting the client through the search process - had a different range of advantages and disadvantages. The main advantage was that more time was spent with the client, which meant that schemes could gain a greater understanding of their particular needs, and so tailor the help accordingly. Simply giving out a list might not be of much help to clients without access to a telephone, or who were unsure about dealing with landlords. The principal disadvantage to offering a supported search service was that it was time consuming, and schemes were more reliant on vacancies being available in the local newspapers or from landlords calling in. If vacancies were not immediately available, then the search might become more protracted.

Matching client and landlord

The next stage in the process of securing accommodation for a client was to match the client with appropriate accommodation or, if the client had found their own accommodation, checking to see that the accommodation chosen was suitable. Three quarters of schemes (75 per cent) always completed an assessment of their clients' general housing and support needs. This assessment often included discussion of the client's housing preferences, size of property required, location, whether furnished or unfurnished, and whether shared or self-contained. Clients were usually advised at the matching stage about what type of property they would be able to afford in that particular area.

Three fifths of schemes (59 per cent) made some assessment of the suitability of the client to take a particular property, which may have been chosen from the approved vacancy list, have been found during the course of a supported search process, or be a property located by the tenant themselves. The scheme manager used the clients' stated preferences as a basis of the assessment but other factors were also considered, the most important of which was the likelihood of a shortfall occurring between the rent charged and the housing benefit payable. Other factors included making sure that the quality of the accommodation was appropriate for the client. Although many of the schemes only accepted properties which met their own defined minimum standards, some schemes commented that they had clients who were more likely to sustain a tenancy in a poor quality property:

> *We also have to recognise that a person may not be able to keep down a nice one-bedroom well-furnished flat, but they may be able to keep down a grotty little bedsit. And if that's all they can keep down, we shouldn't prejudice against that. We should enable them to at least have that and be able to grow from that.*
>
> (Project manager, Westerbury Scheme)

A further important factor, considered for people in HMOs in particular, was the type of people with whom the client might be sharing - whether the house was generally quiet, noisy, smoking or non-smoking, predominantly young people, and if the house had any history of accommodating drug users.

Schemes also made some judgement as to whether the landlord would be suitable for housing a particular client. Some landlords were more relaxed than others about such issues as their tenants keeping the property clean and tidy; noise tolerance; and payments of shortfall. Clients more or less likely to comply with regulations were directed to landlords with appropriate degrees of flexibility. It was also the case that some schemes placed reliance on landlords who were used to dealing with a particular client type. For example, the County Scheme, which often dealt with recovering alcoholics, used a small number of landladies who were familiar with this client group and offered some degree of support with their tenancies.

Although schemes often advised clients on the suitability of particular properties, if a client decided to ignore the advice given and still take a property, then that decision was respected. It was felt to be important that the client should have some say in where they were housed. For this reason, most schemes made the effort to give the client a choice, even if the choice might only be between two properties. Around a quarter of schemes always took clients to view the property before they had to decide whether to take it, and a further 40 per cent of schemes sometimes did so. Only one of the case study schemes consciously limited the choice of properties available, and that was the London Scheme. Clients were made aware that they would only be given once choice of property, and that refusal of that property would only be accepted if a good reason was given. If the client did not like the property, then they had to continue living in temporary accommodation.

In all, schemes considered a degree of involvement in matching tenant and landlord to be a good thing. There was some cautionary comment, however, with respect to having too strong an involvement. It was possible that either the tenant or the landlord might assume that the matching process amounted to a recommendation, implying scheme liability if some problem with the tenancy arose. The Northwest Scheme commented that landlords often wanted some guarantee of clients' good behaviour, and *'they also tend to hold you responsible for anything that* [the clients] *do'*. This was a problem especially encountered by the London Scheme principally, the manager assumed, because the client had only a limited choice of property, and the landlord no choice at all in the client the council placed.

Establishing a sustainable tenancy

Once the client had been found a suitable property, many schemes became involved in setting up the tenancy. Much of the activity under this heading was directed towards ensuring that the tenancy would be sustainable in the long term. Many tenancies break down because the condition of the property is poor; the tenant can not afford the rent; and because tenants, perhaps unaware of their rights, are sometimes unlawfully asked to leave by their landlord. Most schemes offered services at the start of the tenancy, to forestall difficulties which could arise later: vetting properties; negotiating on rent with landlords; and ensuring that legally binding tenancy agreements were signed. Ninety-nine per cent of schemes offered at least one of these services, and 44 per cent offered all.

Vetting properties

In running approved landlords lists, most schemes kept some information on the individual landlords they were dealing with. In addition, checks were also made on specific properties. Half the schemes always visited properties, although there were different stages at which this visit might take place: before the landlord was placed on the register; before the property was offered to the client; or with the client when they were deciding whether to take the tenancy. In half the cases (52 per cent), the schemes always judged the quality of the property by using some sort of minimum standard.

Schemes were asked to detail the sorts of standards they applied, and Table 5.1 summarises the responses. Most schemes which were checking properties used a set of specified standards, usually those applied by the local environmental health office. HMOs were often only used if they had been registered. A number of schemes made specific safety checks on such things as gas and electrical fittings and fire hazards.

Table 5.1
Checks made by schemes on properties

	number of schemes
Complies with environmental health standards	57
HMOs are registered	19
Fire safety	27
Gas fittings	14
Electrical safety	10
Damp	3
(Base = 111)	
Note - more than one response could be given	
Source: postal survey	

Scheme managers were asked how these standards were applied, and there was a wide variety of responses. The London Scheme, for example, looked at space, fitness, dampness and condensation, the quality of the furniture and decoration, and asked the landlord for gas and fire certificates. The Northern Scheme, which tended to include properties at the lower end of the market, focused its checks on smoke and fire alarms, the provision of reasonable quality furniture, adequate heating, general cleanliness and a good standard of decoration, and good conditions in shared kitchens and bathrooms.

Despite the operation of a range of checks, the standard which was most heavily relied upon was a subjective one: would the scheme manager live there themselves? The manager of the Northern Scheme summed up this standard succinctly: *'does your flesh crawl as you walk in or would you be happy to stay there yourself?'*. The same sentiment was expressed by the manager of the London Scheme: *'the rule of thumb we operate is that it should be of a standard that the housing officer themselves would not mind living in'*.

All the scheme managers who made checks were asked what happened when a property did not meet their minimum standard. There were three possible options. One of the schemes rejected the property entirely, and would not include it on the schemes' register, or allow clients access to the vacancy. Three schemes said that they would not issue a guarantee on such a property, although they would not stop a client moving in. The remaining three schemes which vetted properties said that they would advise clients of poor standards, but would not stop them moving in unless the property was a serious health hazard. This flexibility on conditions reflected the limited availability of good quality accommodation, and the desperation of some of the clients in needing to find somewhere immediately. One of the schemes said that they might use sub-standard accommodation as a stop-gap, but would move the client as soon as better quality accommodation was available:

> *you know, they can survive quite well in quite not-good accommodation if they're supported, so we try and make sure that people do get that support, and we keep tabs and we can move them on...to somewhere better as it comes up.*
>
> (Project worker, Northwest Scheme)

Few of the schemes (14 per cent) always referred properties to the environmental health office (EHO) before being accepted onto their scheme. None of the scheme managers interviewed said that they had any formalised relationship with the EHO, and the response to the idea was generally negative. Even the London Scheme, which for the most part applied quite restrictive EHO standards, said that they did not want to involve the EHO directly, since doing so often acted as a disincentive for landlords to become involved in the scheme. Some of the schemes also said that the EHO would be likely to close down some of the properties they were relying on to house their clients, and so exacerbate the shortage of available accommodation. The project worker from the Northwest Scheme commented on involving EHOs: *'Ideally yes, I think it would be a good idea, but on the other hand it's cutting down options'*.

One third of schemes did not apply minimum standards to the properties used, and one fifth did not visit properties. Four of the case study schemes were in this group of 'non-vetting' schemes. The Westerbury Scheme manager considered that the disadvantages attached to vetting outweighed the advantages. For him, applying standards meant that some clients would not get help: *'the more restrictive you get, the narrower the group of people you can assist'*. For another one of the non-vetting schemes, there was less a question of vetting holding disadvantages then such activity simply being unnecessary. The scheme had been very happy with the sort of properties their clients seemed to be finding, and so did not feel it necessary to check. The remaining two schemes did not check properties because they did not have the staff time to do so. Both felt that checking properties would be a valuable addition to their scheme, however. In one of these cases, the manager produced a list for clients to use to check the properties themselves.

In all, schemes generally considered that there was merit in having some system of checking properties, but not one that operated in such a way that landlords felt discouraged from letting. Although schemes were happy to apply their own standards which were in some cases based on environmental health guidelines, actually involving the environmental health office was considered to be a risky strategy since properties might be closed down. Thus decisions on vetting became a question of applying standards, but not standards which were so high that a large proportion of properties would be excluded.

Rent negotiation

Three quarters of schemes (73 per cent) sometimes tried to negotiate down rents with landlord, and one fifth (19 per cent) always did so. Scheme managers commented that they were often in a stronger position than the client to enter into any negotiation on the rent: for example, the Southwest Scheme manager commented: *'I mean, they are not in a position to negotiate with the landlord. They're not the sort of people who can negotiate. They don't have the skills'*. Schemes, in being able to offer a package of services as well as providing a client, thought themselves more likely to be able to bargain for a lower rent. As with most other aspects of help with access, the question of negotiating rents was not a straightforward one. Negotiation was not a static event which took place at a given time in the process of setting up a tenancy. Negotiation could take place at any one of a number of stages, and it was not always likely that the scheme introduced discussion on the rent at the same stage with each landlord.

The earliest stage at which negotiation took place was during the first discussion between the scheme and the landlord - for example, the point at which the landlord contacted the scheme for information. The landlord would perhaps be advised by the scheme what level of rent housing benefit was likely to cover, and that the client would probably not be able to make up any shortfall in the housing benefit payment. Despite the fact that the rent might be low, the landlord may still be persuaded by the scheme to take on clients because the housing benefit payments, once processed, are regular, and the scheme might provide a good supply of tenants. It was clear that case study scheme managers often did not class this sort of discussion as negotiation, even though the result could be a reduced rent for a scheme client.

It was also possible for rents to be discussed at a slightly later stage, when a specific client decided they wanted to move into the landlord's property. This was a process that schemes were more likely to recognise as negotiation. Schemes often tried to make an estimate of what the likely housing benefit payment might be. Negotiation then took place on how much shortfall a client might be able to pay. Shifting focus to the shortfall was evidently a better strategy than getting the landlord to reduce the rent asked for, since many landlords were inflexible on this point:

> *It's very difficult to negotiate with landlords to drop the rent. They have a figure in mind, that's what they want, and at the end of the day there's plenty of people coming round.*
>
> (Scheme worker, Westerbury Scheme)

Occasionally, the client might have lived some time in the property before negotiation took place. This situation may be a consequence of delays in housing benefit payments, which also delayed the tenant and landlord finding out the extent of the shortfall. There were indications that negotiation on the shortfall at this stage was more likely to succeed if the client had proved to be a good tenant who the landlord wanted to keep.

Four of the case study schemes did not negotiate on rents at all. Two of the schemes had no involvement in this side of setting up the tenancy. Of the others, one scheme - the City Scheme - did not even attempt to negotiate because it was thought that the landlords simply would not respond. The remaining scheme - the Churches Scheme - did not negotiate because it was thought that the rents charged were reasonable.

Checking tenancy agreements

Nearly all schemes (93 per cent) sometimes or always explained to the client their tenancy rights and obligations. A smaller proportion of schemes (45 per cent) always examined and approved the tenancy agreement, and a further third sometimes did so. In some cases, the schemes were very closely involved with the legal processes of setting up a tenancy, and this was most likely to be the case where deposit payments were involved. Three of the case study schemes provided model agreements, two of which were six-month shortholds, and one an agreement giving a 12-month shorthold tenancy. None of these schemes made it a requirement that the landlord should accept the scheme's agreement, but the majority of landlords seemed happy to do so.

Four of the schemes were willing to look over the tenancy agreements if the client or landlord requested it, but did not take this action as a matter of course. One scheme - the Townshire Scheme - said that they requested a copy of the agreement for their files, but did not examine it to see if it was a legal one. Two of the schemes had no involvement at all with the agreements.

Conclusion

The process of helping a client find somewhere to live was a complex one, which involved schemes in a number of decisions about the way in which to handle particular tasks. Most schemes kept a landlord register, but that information was not always used directly to help clients. It was more likely to be the case that approved landlord registers, approved vacancy lists and vacancy lists were employed directly to give the client access to a range of available places to stay. Schemes could give only limited assessment of the type of help they gave, since they tended not to have made any conscious assessment of the particular approach they had taken.

Finding somewhere to stay had three elements. Giving the client access to vacancies entailed help which ranged from the simple production of a list, to the project worker giving extended support to the client in the search process. Ensuring a good match between the tenant, the property and the landlord was considered to be an important part of the whole process, although schemes were careful to try and avoid the appearance of having recommended either a tenant or a landlord. The great majority of schemes were also involved in setting up tenancies. Vetting the properties used, negotiating on rents, and checking tenancy agreements were all ways in which schemes tried to ensure that the tenancies would be sustainable.

Chapter Six
Help with Deposits

Introduction

Assistance with deposits is often defined in financial terms, with discussion restricted to assessing the comparative merits of paying cash or issuing guarantees. Analysis of the services provided by schemes, however, illustrates the value of a broader approach to help with deposits. This chapter, therefore, looks in detail at four separate elements which comprised help with bond payments: making out furniture inventories; dealing with the deposit by negotiation with the landlord, paying cash or issuing guarantees; helping with saving; and dealing with the end of the tenancy. The chapter demonstrates that few schemes offered only one approach to dealing with deposits: more tended to offer a mix of strategies.

Furniture inventories

Seventy per cent of all schemes either always or sometimes ensured that a furniture inventory was completed and signed by the tenant and landlord at the beginning of the tenancy. As might be expected, this proportion was much higher amongst schemes offering assistance with the deposit, since they needed documented evidence of furniture and conditions to protect their guarantee funds from false claims. All the case study schemes issuing guarantees undertook furniture inventories. These were usually completed using a form, which had space in which to note property condition as well as listing the furniture and fixtures provided. In all cases, the inventory was signed by the landlord, the tenant and the project manager. There were a few instances where landlords or property agents provided inventories, which schemes checked, but in general terms landlords were happy to have the schemes provide and complete inventories themselves.

There was not a complete correlation between schemes completing inventories, and help with deposit payment, however. A quarter of the schemes completing furniture inventories did not give any sort of financial assistance with deposits. This sort of help can still be regarded as indirect assistance with deposits. These schemes were evidently not completing inventories to protect their own funds, but to protect deposits paid by clients themselves. As has been seen in chapter one, many people have difficulty with landlords who retain deposits unfairly. Completing a furniture inventory reduces landlords' ability to keep back deposits on the pretext of supposed damage or theft, and so perhaps enabling the client to use the returned money as deposit on their next rented property.

Assistance with the deposit

Eighty-one per cent of schemes gave some sort of assistance with the deposit payment itself, by helping in one of three ways: negotiating with the landlord to reduce or waive the payment; paying cash to either the landlord or the tenant; or issuing a guarantee. Table 6.1 indicates the proportion of schemes offering each type of assistance, including those schemes offering both cash and guarantees.

Table 6.1
Assistance given with deposits

Type of assistance	proportion of schemes %
Negotiation only	22
Cash only	27
Guarantees only	39
Cash and guarantees	12
Total	100
(Base = 144 schemes)	
Source: postal survey	

Negotiation on deposits

Although Table 6.1 indicates that just over a fifth of schemes offered only negotiation to assist with deposits, those schemes giving financial help often also tried negotiation in addition to giving financial assistance. Interviews with the case study schemes showed how negotiation worked in practice. The manager of the City Scheme advised all landlords contacting the scheme with available properties that the clients were unlikely to be able to pay a bond. Landlords still insisting on asking for large deposits were excluded from the approved vacancy list. Similarly, the London Scheme, which ran an approved landlord register, only allowed landlords on the register who agreed not to ask the clients for a deposit. The scheme manager had decided not to offer cash assistance at all, because it would counteract the possibility of this sort of negotiation being successful:

> *Landlords will require what you are prepared to give them...If you say to landlords 'We'll pay you deposit and damage guarantees' they'll say thank you very much and then insist on them.*
> (Scheme manager, London Scheme)

Two of the case study schemes not running approved landlord registers, but undertaking a supported search service, helped by negotiating with landlords on behalf of particular clients. Both schemes considered that this approach had been fairly successful, and each had a reasonable record of persuading landlords to take deposits which the clients paid in weekly instalments.

Some schemes offering guarantees also tried to negotiate with the landlord on the requirement to pay a deposit. For example, the Northern Scheme did not volunteer the guarantee until the landlord actually asked for a deposit. This approach was felt to be more successful if the landlord had contacted the scheme with a vacancy, and was evidently eager to get the vacancy filled as soon as possible. One of the schemes offering a guarantee, however, did not negotiate on principle, since it was considered to be important that possible costs to the landlord should be acknowledged, and that it would be unfair to leave the landlord without some degree of financial cover.

Although schemes' trying to negotiate on the deposit was a common approach, the tactic carried one major disadvantage: it tended to exclude landlords offering good standard accommodation, as one scheme worker commented:

> *...the more money and facilities a landlord's going to put into a property, the more they're going to want to protect that investment by...wanting rent in advance and deposits.*
> (Scheme worker, Northwest Scheme)

For the two schemes with a good record of negotiating down deposits, the success of negotiation rested to a large degree on them having built up a relationship with landlords at the bottom end of their local rental market, where landlords were already flexible on deposits and tended to ask for relatively small sums of money. This sort of landlord was more likely to allow negotiation on the reduction of a deposit or to accept a sum in instalments.

...there are some that just sort of want maybe £100 deposit and sometimes I can negotiate it down to, say, £50 and maybe young people can actually manage to get that from relatives or whatever you know.

(Scheme worker, Northwest Scheme)

Landlords further up the market, however, were less willing to negotiate their deposits:

...if they're asking for four weeks' rent in advance and four weeks rent in advance as a deposit, then I know that they're basically not going to come down to nothing.

(Scheme worker, Northwest Scheme)

Cash help with deposits

Just over a quarter of schemes gave cash assistance with deposits, actually paying the deposit money on behalf of the client. Cash deposit schemes were more likely to have been set up earlier than schemes issuing guarantees: half of the cash deposit schemes had been set up by 1992, but three quarters of guarantee schemes were set up in the three years 1993-5. The two chronologies are probably connected: the decline in the number of schemes giving cash help with deposits was no doubt a consequence of the growing popularity of the issue of guarantees. The majority of the cash deposit schemes (64 per cent) helped by giving the deposit money directly to the landlord. A small number - only three - gave the money to the client. Eleven schemes gave the money to either the landlord or the client.

Two of the case study schemes gave cash assistance with deposits. The Churches Scheme gave a cash deposit to the landlord, who was expected to return the money at the end of the tenancy. The Townshire Scheme required its clients to find accommodation by using a local property agent. The scheme worker personally handed over a cheque to the agent to cover the cost of the deposit.

In general terms there was perceived to be only one advantage to giving cash assistance with deposits: it was thought to be more acceptable to landlords. The disadvantages were considered to be substantial, however. Schemes reported difficulties in recovering their cash payments from both landlords and clients at the end of tenancies.

Deposit guarantees

Two fifths of all schemes helping with deposits - 39 per cent - did so by only issuing guarantees. A further 12 per cent also issued guarantees, but operated in such a way that they sometimes gave cash. On average, schemes had issued guarantees to the value of 35 per cent of their guarantee fund. This low proportion was perhaps a reflection of the fact that many of the schemes had not been operating for very long at the time of the postal survey. Eighty per cent of the schemes operating in 1993/4 gave guarantees for 30 clients or less. The average number issued was 22, but this figure excludes the small number of schemes which had not yet issued any guarantees - perhaps because their schemes were not particularly popular - and three exceptional schemes which had each issued over 150 guarantees. The average value of a 1993/4 guarantee was £242.

Each of the guarantees had four separate elements: a maximum value; a specified period for which the guarantee was valid; a defined set of eventualities covered; and a strategy for dealing with the ending of the time limit. Each of these elements will be discussed in turn. Table 6.2 shows the maximum amounts covered by guarantees.

Table 6.2
Maximum amounts covered by guarantees

amount	number of schemes
£100	7
£101-200	6
£201-300	15
£301-400	7
£401-500	4
4 weeks' rent	27
No maximum specified	5
(Base = 71 schemes)	
Source: postal survey	

The largest proportion of schemes did not specify an actual cash amount for their maximum payment, but instead indicated that their guarantees' maximum covered up to the equivalent value of four weeks' rent on any individual tenancy. Five per cent of the schemes did not specify any maximum payment. Taking only those schemes giving a numeric maximum, the average maximum guarantee was £260. As has been seen, above, the average value of guarantees issued tended to be slightly lower than the average specified maximum (£242 compared with £260).

The majority of guarantee schemes (53 per cent) issued guarantees to cover a period of six months. Just over a quarter had no maximum time period, and issued guarantees which were intended to last for the full length of the tenancy. Seventeen per cent of schemes had guarantees lasting a full year, and a small proportion (two per cent) issued guarantees lasting two years.

All the guarantees covered damage done to the property by the client, and 79 per cent also covered theft. There was less agreement about whether the guarantee should cover other contingencies. Just under half of the schemes (47 per cent) issued guarantees which covered rent arrears, and slightly less issued guarantees which compensated the landlord for rent in lieu of notice. Taking 'packages' of contingencies together, half the guarantees only covered either damage or damage and theft, and a third covered damage, theft, rent arrears and rent in lieu of notice.

At the end of the period the guarantee was expected to cover, schemes took either one of two possible courses of action. The majority of schemes (74 per cent) offered a renewable guarantee, which meant that the guarantee could continue cover for another time period. Just under half of these schemes did not renew automatically, but made an assessment of the tenancy, which meant that renewal depended on the circumstances of the client and the attitude of the landlord. For example, in cases where the landlord was happy to continue the tenancy without deposit cover, then the guarantee was withdrawn. Some schemes only continued cover if the client was saving to cover the cost of the deposit themselves, but had not saved quite enough. By contrast, just over a quarter of guarantee schemes (26 per cent) had a definite time limit on guarantee coverage. At the end of the time period, an assessment would be made of any claim from the landlord, and the scheme would withdraw. Clients were then expected to deal with providing a deposit themselves.

The diversity of approaches to guarantees is illustrated by the examples of the case study schemes, four of which regularly issued guarantees. The Southwest Scheme had a guarantee with a maximum value of four times the weekly rent, covering damage, rent in arrears, rent in lieu of notice and theft. The guarantee was valid for a maximum of six months, although this could be extended if the client had saved regularly to cover the cost of the deposit but had not saved enough. If the client was not saving, then the scheme informed landlord and client that the guarantee had lapsed. The Westerbury Scheme gave a guarantee which also had a maximum value of one month's rent, but only covered damage and theft. The guarantee was renewable after its six-month period had come to a close. The Charity Scheme was again different. Its maximum guarantee value was £450, but only covered damage. The guarantee was valid for six months, but was renewable for an additional six months. After that time, however, it was withdrawn. The Northern Scheme offered a guarantee with a maximum payment of £200, covering damage, rent in arrears, rent in lieu of notice (limited to one week only) and theft. Like the Charity

Scheme, the Northern Scheme's guarantee covered six months and had a further six month's extension period after which time it was withdrawn.

In evaluating the merits of issuing deposits, schemes often mentioned that they had considered offering cash, but that guarantees had appeared to be a much better option. Although some thought that landlords might prefer cash, schemes generally considered that if a landlord operated lawfully, then it should make no difference whether the deposit was paid in cash or guarantee form:

> *...the main concern I had in the beginning was that it would mean a loss of properties available to us. No doubt we have lost properties, but we've also made other contacts. If a landlord works in an appropriate way there should be no difference.*
>
> (Scheme worker, Westerbury Scheme)

For some schemes, a major advantage was that the deposit fund was not constantly depleted by the inability to recover deposit cash from landlords or tenants. The cash went even further for one of the case study schemes, which issued guarantees in excess of the bond funds available, on the basis of only paying out a tenth of their cash each year in claims. The main disadvantage of issuing guarantees related to the burden of administrative work. This was especially the case where guarantees were renewable, and where clients could transfer the bond from one property to another. Both eventualities entailed visits to the properties and checks being made to the inventory. Schemes gave little assessment of the relative merits of different types of guarantee, although the Westerbury Scheme manager said that he was unhappy that their guarantee only covered damage and theft. This issue was one which landlords were very much concerned about, as will be seen in chapter ten.

Help with saving

A further feature in those schemes where cover was time-limited, was whether clients were helped in saving to finance the bond themselves when the scheme's cover expired. Sixteen per cent of the schemes giving help with deposits also ran a system whereby clients could save, so that they could pay the deposit themselves when the cover offered by the scheme ran out. This sort of help was given by both guarantee and cash deposit schemes, but was slightly more common amongst schemes giving cash help, where the assistance given could more easily be described as a loan.

Five of the case study schemes said that they gave some encouragement to their clients to save to cover the cost of the deposit. Two of the schemes which gave cash help with deposits expected the clients to save, although the way in which the savings interacted with the help given varied slightly in each case. The Churches Deposit Scheme gave assistance by paying a cash deposit to the landlord, which was expected to cover a specified time period. Clients were encouraged to save to cover the cost of the deposit themselves, since at the end of the cover period, the scheme required repayment of the deposit back from the landlord. The Townshire Borough Council Deposit Scheme was much more formalised, and essentially comprised a loan agreement between the tenant and the council. The Scheme paid the deposit to the property agent on behalf of the client, who then had to pay the money back to the council in specified instalments. The repayments were arranged through the council's legal department, which actively pursued the scheme's bad debtors.

Three of the case study schemes issuing guarantees encouraged their clients to save, but two offered no help in doing so. By contrast, the Southwest Scheme had set up a special pay-in account with a local bank, and gave pay-in books to their clients with guarantees. Clients were expected to save £1 a week. At the time of the interview with the project manager, the Scheme had 20 per cent of its clients involved in saving, but hoped to increase this proportion to 80 per cent. Savings were not always regularly made, but where the client was evidently making an effort to put money by, the scheme allowed the guarantee to continue providing cover until the full cost of the deposit was saved.

Although many schemes considered that instituting any sort of saving scheme would entail far too much time in chasing tenants for money, the Southwest Scheme thought that there were advantages beyond the fact that money was being repaid into the guarantee fund:

> We find that people who save...they don't even want to lose £10, you know, of their money. It doesn't matter how much, our risk effectively drops to a very low figure, I was going to say nil but it's a bit more than that, but our risk drops right down once they start saving.
>
> (Scheme manager, Southwest Scheme)

Thus even a small amount of saving increased the clients' stake in the tenancy and determination for it to succeed.

Dealing with the end of the tenancy

Nearly half the schemes which gave no help with the payment of deposit money still gave indirect assistance with bonds by negotiating with landlords for the repayment of deposits from a client's previous tenancy. For example, the Metropolitan Scheme, because of its experience of advocacy work, was often involved in representing clients in cases where deposits had been unfairly retained by the landlord.

It was much more commonly the case, however, that schemes became involved in claims against deposits when they themselves had dealt with payment of the deposit. In cases where a cash payment had been made to the landlord, the scheme would approach the landlord for repayment, and negotiate on any claims for compensation. Schemes would then try and pursue the client to cover the cost of valid claims by landlords.

Where guarantees had been issued, it was up to the landlord to approach the scheme for compensation. In these cases, the scheme would complete a second inventory, to compare with the first, and then agree an appropriate payment. Only a small number of schemes operating in 1993/4 had issued guarantees with no claims being made. On average, guarantee schemes each dealt with eight claims on which payments were agreed. The highest average payment made out by a scheme on claims was £375, and the lowest £33. Taking all schemes together, the overall average claim was £180.

Information on the proportion of guarantee funds being paid out in claims in 1993/4 was available for 22 schemes. On average, 10 per cent of funds were paid out in claims. As with the cash deposit schemes, guarantee schemes would sometimes try and pursue the client for payments on the bond. Discussion with scheme managers on this issue, however, showed that schemes tended not to chase clients particularly vigorously. Most simply said that if a client incurred payment out of the guarantee fund, then they would not be helped again.

Conclusion

This chapter has demonstrated that help with deposit payments was not restricted to cash or guarantee assistance but could include negotiation and other services which helped a client recover any deposit from their last tenancy. Most schemes offered a range of help with deposits, although the majority helping with the payment of the deposit itself did so by issuing guarantees. This option was seen as being largely preferable to giving cash assistance. An average guarantee valued £242, lasted six months but was renewable, and covered theft and damage. However, this generalisation should not be allowed to disguise the wide degree of variety in the nature of the guarantees issued: some could be limited both financially and in terms of the contingencies covered, and others could cover a wide range of eventualities.

Chapter Seven
Help with Housing Benefit and Rent in Advance

Introduction

This chapter looks at help given with housing benefit and with rent in advance. Almost all schemes gave some help with housing benefit, and this chapter shows that schemes offered one of three packages of services, each of which had a different level of assistance. The chapter also explores help given with rent in advance. In the same way that help with deposits did not always comprise cash payments or the issue of guarantees, help with rent in advance often included non-financial activities such as help in making social fund claims and negotiation with the landlord to reduce or waive the requirement to pay.

The chapter examines rent in advance and housing benefit services together, since a scheme's ability to help with rent in advance was often dependent on some degree of involvement with the client's housing benefit application. Indeed, the chapter will conclude that one of the more common approaches to help with rent in advance was to negotiate away this requirement on the strength of offering services which speeded up housing benefit payments.

Help with housing benefit

Ninety-eight per cent of schemes gave some sort of assistance with housing benefit, and four particular services were defined. First, and most popular, was offering the client advice on housing benefit and help with completing the application form. Almost all schemes - 98 per cent - always or sometimes offered this service, with the intention of both helping the client with the form, and speeding up the application by making sure that the form had been completed correctly. All the case study schemes, apart from the Townshire Scheme, gave assistance by offering to complete the application form with the client, and by ensuring that all the relevant information was sent with the form. In some cases the schemes kept copies of the application form ready for clients to complete, and also had proforma letters which landlords could use to provide the necessary information on the tenancy. Some schemes photocopied the applications to keep on file, and delivered the applications themselves to the housing benefit office.

Second, nine in 10 schemes always or sometimes arranged for the housing benefit payment to be sent directly to the landlord. This arrangement had to be made with the agreement of clients who are, by law, free to decide for themselves where cheques should be sent. Schemes often made this requirement for two reasons: landlords often preferred housing benefit to be paid directly; and it was felt to be more helpful for clients not to be faced with the temptation of receiving large cheques. As the worker from the Northwest Scheme commented: '...*quite often they're quite happy to pay the rent, it's just that they have such a small amount of money, it's very easy to be robbing Peter to pay Paul'*. For the most part, clients preferred to have the payments made directly to the landlord, and complied with schemes' suggestions for this to be the case. Two of the case study schemes - the London Scheme and the Southwest Scheme were more prescriptive. These schemes made the direct payment of housing benefit to the landlord a requirement that clients had to comply with, to be entitled to help from them.

Third, just under half the schemes (47 per cent) operated a 'fast-track' agreement with the housing benefit office to ensure that the client's applications were processed within a given time. Seventy per cent of the fast-tracking schemes had arranged for payments to be processed within the statutory period of 14 days. The remainder - possibly working in areas where housing benefit processing was slow - promised payment within four weeks. Only two of the case study schemes had fast-track agreements with their housing benefit office. The London Scheme had a specified officer dealing with scheme applications, and promised that applications would be completed within four to six weeks - this in an area where applications were notoriously slow to be processed. The Churches Scheme also had a nominated officer in the benefits office dealing with scheme claims, and so offering faster processing. For the majority of the remaining schemes, setting up a fast-track system was not considered necessary, since claims - so long as they were completed correctly - were already being processed within the statutory time limit. One of the case study managers did not set up a fast-track system on principle, since she did not think that her clients should get priority over other people who might be in just as severe housing need.

Fourth, once the application had been submitted, 90 per cent of schemes always or sometimes offered to liaise between the tenant/landlord and the housing benefit office should any difficulties arise. Most of the case study schemes gave continuing help with housing benefit. In most cases, this help included chasing applications where payments had been delayed. For example, the Metropolitan Scheme routinely told its clients to return to the scheme office two weeks after an application had been submitted, and the scheme would telephone the benefits office to see how far the application had progressed.

Extended housing benefit help also included conducting appeals against housing benefit levels which incurred heavy shortfall payments, and dealing with problems arising from tenants' changes of circumstances.

Not all schemes offered all four sorts of help. Three groupings of services emerged, as Table 7.1 demonstrates.

Table 7.1
Types of help given with housing benefit

Type of help	Proportion of schemes		
	All	Voluntary Sector schemes	Local Authority schemes
	%	%	%
Advice and initial help with form only	7	5	13
Extended assistance with application	46	49	40
Fast-tracked application	46	46	47
Total	99	100	100
(Base)	(157)	(45)	(112)
NB - percentages may not total 100 due to rounding			
Source: postal survey			

As Table 7.1 shows, a small proportion of all schemes - seven per cent - restricted their help simply to dealing with the initial housing benefit form, and making sure that the housing benefit would be paid directly to the landlord. Forty-six per cent of the schemes helped with the initial application, but extended their help further into the application process by liaising, when necessary, with the housing benefit office. A third group of schemes - also 46 per cent - offered initial help and continued support but also included a fast-track agreement.

Table 7.1 also gives the type of housing benefit help given according to scheme status. The table shows that fast-tracked housing benefit systems were equally likely to have been established by local authority and voluntary sector agencies. However, local authority schemes were slightly less likely than voluntary sector schemes to be offering extended help, and it was more commonly the case that local authority help consisted only of giving initial support with the housing benefit form.

Deciding on which sort of help to give with housing benefit was evidently very dependent on the speed with which the benefit was processed in a given area. It was not always necessary for schemes to give extended or fast-tracked help with housing benefit, in places where processing took place within the statutory time period. It was also the case that some schemes did not offer extended help because they were working with landlords used to accommodating delays with benefit payments.

Help with rent in advance

Eighty-nine per cent of schemes gave some sort of help with rent in advance. Four types of help were defined under this general heading: helping the client make an application to the social fund; negotiating with the landlord to reduce or waive rent in advance; making a single cash payment of rent in advance; and paying the rent until the housing benefit was processed - a service which might or might not include a payment of rent in advance. Table 7.2 indicates the proportion of schemes taking each of these approaches.

Table 7.2
Help given with rent in advance

Help given	Proportion of schemes		
	All	Local Authority	Voluntary Sector
	%	%	%
No help	12	17	11
Application to the social fund only	3	2	3
Negotiation only	53	46	56
Single cash payment of rent in advance	15	23	11
Paying rent until HB processed	17	12	19
Total	100	100	100
(Base)	(161)	(48)	(113)
Source: postal survey			

Table 7.2 shows that, taking all schemes together, 12 per cent gave no help at all with rent in advance. Local authority schemes were less likely than voluntary sector schemes to give help with rent in advance.

Applying to the social fund

In total, 47 per cent of schemes always or sometimes helped a client to apply to the social fund for money to pay rent in advance, although only three per cent of schemes offered this as the only help they gave with rent in advance help. Schemes were much more likely to use application to the social fund as an additional strategy, especially in cases where their main strategy was to try and negotiate with the landlord.

Two of the case study schemes applied to the social fund fairly regularly. The County Scheme routinely encouraged its clients to apply, and supported appeals when applications had been unsuccessful. The Metropolitan Scheme kept social fund application forms which clients could complete with the help of scheme staff. This scheme was located in a local authority area where payments out of the social fund for rent in advance were reasonably common. Four other schemes encouraged clients to apply, but said that the success rate was very low.

Application to the social fund for rent in advance help was generally seen to carry more disadvantages than advantages, even in areas where payments were common. If help was given, it was generally made in the form of a loan, which the client had to pay back. Perhaps more importantly, however, was the fact that some schemes considered that it was better for some clients not to apply to the social fund for rent in advance, since they might also need help with furniture or kitchen equipment. According to one scheme manager, *'You only get one bite at the cherry'*: the social fund did not often give more than one loan at any one time and since landlords were often open to negotiation, it was best to use social fund applications to pay for necessary household items.

Negotiation

Dealing with rent in advance by negotiating with the landlord was a popular strategy, even amongst the schemes which also offered cash assistance. In total, 80 per cent of schemes tried negotiation always or some of the time, and 53 per cent of schemes relied on negotiation alone. As Table 7.2 shows, this strategy tended to be relied on by more voluntary sector schemes than local authority schemes.

As with deposits, negotiation on rent in advance could take place at the time of the initial contact between the landlord and the scheme. For example, the London Scheme only took landlords onto its approved landlord register if they agreed not to ask for rent in advance. Other schemes tended to try and negotiate on rent in advance on behalf of particular clients. Project managers generally felt that landlords were more flexible about rent in advance if they had assurances that the actual rent would be paid quickly. Schemes had responded to this attitude by developing a wider degree of assistance with housing benefit applications. Providing this sort of service meant that, even if rent in advance was not being paid, the schemes could still give the landlord some guarantee that they would receive housing benefit within a given time period. This strategy was common amongst all the schemes which relied on negotiation to deal with rent in advance. Compared with schemes giving cash assistance, negotiating schemes were nearly twice as likely to have set up fast-track housing benefit systems.

Cash payments of rent in advance

Twenty-two per cent of schemes gave cash assistance with rent in advance, with 15 per cent of schemes having this as their main type of help. Schemes giving this sort of assistance often felt that giving cash help was the only way in which landlords could be persuaded to take scheme clients. Giving cash help with rent in advance was more common amongst local authority schemes than with voluntary sector schemes. Nearly a quarter of local authorities (23 per cent) were giving this sort of help, compared with just over a tenth of voluntary sector schemes (11 per cent).

In essence, cash help for rent in advance was a loan given by the scheme to the client, on the security of the first housing benefit cheque. In the majority of cases, the scheme gave a cheque to the landlord, and arranged with the client for the scheme to receive the first housing benefit cheque. A small number of schemes gave the cash to the client, and required reimbursement directly from the client. Only one of the case study schemes gave help with rent in advance by making single payments. The City Scheme paid a cheque covering the first two weeks' rent to the landlord, and then required the client to instruct the housing benefit office to pay the first two weeks' housing benefit back to the scheme.

Rent payments

Seventeen per cent schemes giving help with rent in advance actually took on payment of the rent until the housing benefit application was processed - a payment which sometimes included a sum for rent in advance. Rent payment was more commonly a service offered by voluntary sector schemes compared with local authority schemes (19 per cent compared with 12 per cent). It should perhaps be stressed that the rent payment schemes should not be confused with rent guarantee schemes. These sorts of scheme imply that a landlord's rent is guaranteed over a specified time period, whether or not a tenant is in the property.

The rent payment schemes, on the other hand, were effectively offering loans, although these were over a longer term. Some of the schemes had a limit of four weeks on the amount of time they would continue to pay the rent; others, however, simply continued to pay for as long as was necessary. In all cases, however, the schemes required that they should be paid the first housing benefit cheque. One of the case study schemes offered this sort of help. The Charity Scheme started paying the rent when the client moved in. The scheme also dealt with the housing benefit application, requiring the client to specify that the first benefit cheque should be paid directly to the scheme. The scheme continued to pay the rent and receive the housing benefit until the benefit payments became regular, at which time the housing benefit cheques were diverted to the landlord. The scheme expected the whole process to take up to six months.

The scheme gave this sort of help because it was thought that this would be the only way in which landlords could be persuaded to take on the scheme's clients. The scheme was working in an area where there had been no history of the private rented sector accommodating people on low income, and landlords were generally uncertain about taking housing benefit claimants. None of the other case study schemes had considered taking this approach to help with rent in advance, probably because the combination of negotiation and help with housing benefit had been proving to be reasonably successful.

Conclusion

This chapter has looked at the sorts of help given with housing benefit and the requirement to pay rent in advance. It has shown that schemes could offer one of three types of assistance with rent in advance: help with the initial application; extended help beyond the application, including liaising with the housing benefit office; and arranging a fast-tracked housing benefit payment. Not all schemes considered extended help necessary, since in some areas, the processing of housing benefit was relatively quick.

The majority of schemes offering some help with rent in advance relied on negotiation with the landlord. The chapter showed that negotiating schemes were more likely to have developed extended or fast-tracked help with housing benefit, to enable them to give assurances to landlords that the rent would be paid quickly. This sort of development is a clear indication that help with housing benefit was also considered to be, indirectly, a strategy for dealing with rent in advance. However, financial help with rent in advance was thought to be necessary in areas where landlords had no experience of accommodating people on low incomes.

Chapter Eight
Tenancy Support

Introduction

For the majority of schemes, the offer of help did not finish with setting up a tenancy and dealing with any advance payments. Visits after the start of the tenancy were made to both clients and landlords at least in some cases by three quarters of schemes. This sort of service was aimed at ensuring that tenancies were sustained, and will be referred to in this chapter as 'tenancy support'. The help given included making sure that the tenant had settled in, for example, and dealing with disputes between tenant and landlord. Although most schemes focused their tenancy support on helping the client, supporting the landlord was also a feature. This chapter first looks at tenancy support from the angle of help given to the client, and clarifies the distinction between resettlement and tenancy support. The chapter then examines assistance given to the landlord. The way in which schemes dealt with the end of tenancies is also explored. The chapter begins by defining the types of schemes giving tenancy support.

Schemes and tenancy support

Tenancy support was felt by the majority of schemes to be an important part of their work. As the Charity Scheme manager commented: *'You don't just dump the clients in and run away'*. It was considered to be worth taking the time to ensure that both the landlord and the client were happy with tenancy which had been created. However, this sort of activity was much more common amongst some groups of schemes than others. Table 8.1 indicates the proportions of schemes always or sometimes visiting clients and landlords after the start of a tenancy, according to the schemes' status.

Table 8.1 shows that it was less common for local authority schemes to continue visiting clients or landlords after the start of a tenancy. This finding could be explained by the fact that local authority schemes may have felt that visits were unnecessary: local authority schemes tended not to deal with clients with any sort of special need, and placed more stringent restrictions on the landlords and standard of properties used. Both these factors implied a reduced likelihood that the tenancy would break down.

Table 8.1
Proportion of schemes always or sometimes visiting clients and landlords, according to scheme status

	Proportion of schemes		
	All %	Local Authority schemes %	Voluntary Sector schemes %
Client visit	77	47	89
(Base)	(159)	(47)	(112)
Landlord visit	76	50	87
(Base)	(157)	(46)	(111)
Source: postal survey			

Neither of the case study schemes which were run by local authorities continued visiting either the tenant or the landlord after tenancies had been set up: neither schemes considered such visits necessary, or even appropriate. The London Scheme drew a comparison between its work and placing people in social housing:

> *You don't offer resettlement support for people going into permanent council tenancies: they have basic management support in the tenancy. We would not take any different view for people placed into the private rented sector: there's no reason why we should.*
> (Scheme manager, London Scheme)

Although the scheme's approach was non-interventionary, the manager commented that 'basic management' for its clients placed in the private rented sector included the scheme sorting out any difficulties arising between tenant and landlord on issues such as repairs.

Tenancy support and clients

Table 8.1 indicated that, taken together, the majority of schemes continue to visit tenants after accommodation had been secured for them. It might be possible to interpret this sort of activity as resettlement work, but there are two reasons why this inference should not be drawn. The first reason was that scheme clients tended not to need resettlement. As has been seen in Chapter three, schemes often focused their activity on helping clients who were capable of living independently, and who had limited support needs. According to the Charity Scheme, *'The majority that I've seen since I've been here...they need help to get in,* [and] *there's not really much aftercare that you need to do with them'*. Other schemes echoed this opinion. The County Scheme said, of its clients: *'They just need some help to find somewhere and once they've got it they're fine'*. The City Scheme made a similar comment: *'...it's very easy to forget the people that you just found accommodation, took a few weeks to settle in, and then never really want to see you again'*.

A second reason for scheme work not being regarded as resettlement was that schemes themselves were very clear on the boundaries of the help they were willing to give. For example, the case study schemes did sometimes help clients referred from the probation services, from the social services department, or from hostels. In all cases, however, the agencies making the referral were expected to provide appropriate packages of support. When a client self-referring to the scheme had problems, schemes contacted specialist counselling or addiction workers. Schemes themselves considered that their purpose was to help with access to accommodation, and that they did not have the training or the resources to be of help in other areas:

> *...it's a matter of reducing the work that we don't have to do - that other authorities or voluntary groups are there to do - so that we can concentrate more on the work that we are here to do.*
>
> (Project manager, Westerbury Scheme)

Recourse to other agencies was therefore common, and schemes were evidently geared up to draw in this help when necessary. Eighty per cent of schemes sometimes or always arranged support for the clients they helped.

Although schemes did not resettle clients, other services were provided which were intended to help clients settle into and sustain their tenancies. There were four types of help which could be given. Just over half of schemes always or sometimes helped a client actually move their possessions into the new property. This was perhaps more likely to be the case where a client was moving from temporary hostel accommodation, and had possessions which did not include furniture but were bags and boxes which the scheme worker could take in their car. A service associated with help moving possessions was the offer of furniture, bedding or kitchen equipment, for clients moving into unfurnished tenancies. None of the schemes themselves had furniture stores, but some were being managed by parent organisations which had this resource.

A second service was the offering of independent living and/or budgeting advice. Nearly three quarters of schemes gave this help to all or some of their clients. In discussing this aspect of their work with case study schemes, it was clear that the range of advice given could be quite broad, but tended to focus on financial help which included applying for benefits such as social fund claims for furniture, and setting up budget schemes to pay for heating and electricity. Other sorts of help could include discussing employment and educational options.

As has already been seen, three quarters of schemes continued to visit all or some of the clients they had moved into the property. Six of the case study schemes made client visits. For the most part, these visits were made to ensure that the client had moved in satisfactorily, and had everything they needed. The visits could be quite intensive for the first few days or weeks, but this period was expected to be short-lived. In none of the cases where visits were made was the whole process formalised into any sort of 'contract' between the scheme and the client, but followed the scheme managers' intuitive understanding of the client's need for help. The manager of the City Scheme said that the scheme's approach was dictated by the client:

> *...if I'd, say, arranged to go round for a couple of weeks and if it seemed the people just weren't interested, then I'd maybe leave it for quite a while and ask them to get in touch with me; while if somebody said 'Are you coming here next week' then I would, so it's really client-led.*
> (Scheme manager, City Scheme)

A fourth aspect of tenancy support was that schemes negotiated between the tenant and the landlord on such issues as repairs and arrears. Eighty per cent of schemes gave this sort of help always or sometimes, and almost all the case study schemes could relate instances where this negotiation had been useful. For example, the London Scheme had resolved a dispute between a landlord and client over the cost of putting in a telephone line. The Metropolitan Scheme gave legal advice to tenants on landlords' responsibilities to effect repairs, and offered advocacy services should cases have to go to court. The County Scheme had cleared up at least one disagreement between a landlord and a scheme client which had threatened to end the tenancy.

Tenancy support and landlords

Most case study schemes considered that it was more appropriate to focus their main tenancy support through helping the client, but almost all schemes also offered support to the landlord. Table 8.1 has already shown that three quarters of schemes continue to visit landlords after the start of tenancies. This contact allowed the scheme to keep the landlord up to date on the housing benefit application, for example, or to give assurances that the client was settling in satisfactorily. The landlord might also use this contact as an opportunity to bring up any difficulties they might have been having with a particular tenant.

Table 8.2 indicates the proportions of schemes providing the landlord with other services.

Table 8.2
Proportions of schemes giving types of help to landlords

Type of help	Proportion of schemes %
General tenancy advice	97
Information packs	63
Training	3
Advice on planning applications	21
(Base)	(158)
Note - more than one type of help could be given	
Source: postal survey	

As Table 8.2 shows, most schemes offered advice, and some prepared information which was distributed in packs sent to landlords. Just over a third of schemes were able to give training to landlords on such areas as tenancy law, and a fifth of schemes gave advice on planning applications.

The range of services which was evident in responses to the postal survey was not reflected in activity amongst the case study schemes. Nearly all the schemes gave advice to landlords, but this was largely concentrated in answering queries about housing benefit. Two schemes were slightly exceptional in the advice they gave. The Metropolitan Scheme tried to raise awareness of good practice in its advice to landlords, and the Northern Scheme was prepared to advise on a wider range of matters including environmental health legislation and property grants. Beyond the giving of advice, however, the case study schemes often had little contact with landlords, and none gave landlord training or were involved in advising on planning applications.

Almost all the case study schemes said that they spent much more time with clients than with landlords. This was with the exception of the London Scheme, which perhaps met each landlord two or three times in the course of vetting their property for inclusion on its register. The manager of the Northern Scheme said that she would like to spend more time with landlords, but *'they don't turn up on your doorstep having a crisis as clients do'*. Only one scheme expressed some degree of caution on giving more support to landlords. The Metropolitan Scheme said that becoming more involved with landlords increased the chance that cases of 'split loyalties' might arise. For example, the scheme had given a couple information on a particular vacancy. The landlord was happy with the tenancy initially, but the couple had got into bad company, and had started to deal in drugs, so upsetting other tenants in the shared house. The landlord had returned to the scheme for advice on immediate eviction, but the scheme could only comment that it would have to advise the tenants that they could legally remain in the property until the required notice had elapsed. This particular incident had alienated the landlord, who was unlikely to let to scheme clients again.

The ending of tenancies

Although schemes were, for the most part, focused on setting up and supporting tenancies, many were also involved in tenancies which had come to an end. Only one of the case study schemes said they made a point of trying to find out why tenancies had ended. The scheme angled its help towards resolving any dispute between tenant and landlord, but was not often successful. Schemes were often more formally involved if they had given cash or guarantees to cover bond payments. In these instances, landlords were either expected to return cash deposits or to make a claim against the guarantee.

Almost all the schemes - just over 90 per cent - always or sometimes found their clients somewhere else to live if a scheme tenancy had terminated. Most of the case study scheme managers said that they would help their clients find another property, but only if there had been no difficulties with the scheme tenancy which had just ended. Two of the case study scheme managers said that they never helped clients a second time. In each case, these were schemes giving assistance with bonds. The Townshire Scheme, giving a cash loan for bonds, said that clients should not need to be helped a second time, since they should be able to recover their first bond from the landlord. The Southwest Scheme, which gave bond guarantees and expected its clients to save, said that they also expected clients to be able to recover their bonds, and that helping clients a second time made the scheme look like *'a soft touch'*.

Conclusion

This chapter has shown that almost all the schemes gave some sort of assistance in maintaining a tenancy once it had been set up. Much of this help was concentrated in the first few days or weeks of the tenancy, in ensuring that clients had settled in and had everything they needed. Schemes might also give advice to the client on benefits and budgeting. Once a tenancy was under way, schemes were also available to resolve disputes between tenant and landlord. Although much of the tenancy support was focused on the client, schemes also helped landlords by offering advice and information and keeping in touch during the course of the tenancy should any problems arise. When tenancies terminated, the majority of schemes were willing to help the client into another property.

Section Three

Clients' and Landlords'
Evaluation of Help with Access

Chapter Nine
Clients

Introduction

Section two has described the help given by access schemes, and offered some degree of analysis from the point of view of scheme managers. This chapter will evaluate help with access from the clients' points of view. There will be three parts to the evaluation: clients' responses to individual services, such as help finding somewhere to stay and help with advance payments; their overall assessment of the scheme they were helped by; and an analysis of whether clients were willing to stay in the tenancies created. The chapter will begin with a descriptive summary of the clients who were interviewed.

Characteristics of clients

A total of 39 clients were interviewed from five case study schemes: the Westerbury Scheme, the County Scheme, the London Scheme, the Metropolitan Scheme and the Charity Scheme. All the clients interviewed had been helped by a scheme to secure accommodation in the private rented sector, and in almost all cases were still in those tenancies at the time of the interview. Detailed tables giving the personal characteristics of the clients is given in Appendix two. To summarise, the majority were white, male and over the age of 26. Twenty-one were single with no children and twelve were lone parents. Six of the clients were living with their partner, and five of the couples had dependent children. Twenty-nine of the clients were unemployed, 22 of which had been unemployed for more than a year. Most of the clients were on income support, and all except one received housing benefit.

Almost all the clients had come into contact with schemes at a time of housing need, rather than being in a situation of actual rooflessness. Fifteen of the clients had been in some sort of temporary accommodation, either in hostels or bed and breakfast hotels. Seven had been living with friends or relatives and had been asked to leave. Thirteen of the clients were moving on from what had been fairly settled housing situations. Ten of these had been in private rented sector tenancies which had terminated - most often because the landlord had defaulted on the rented property's mortgage. One of the clients had been in owner occupation, but had lost their job and had had their house repossessed. Two had been in council or housing association tenancies, and had been forced to leave: one because of domestic violence, and one because of harassment from neighbourhood children. Four of the clients had been in situations which could be classed as roofless: two of these had been sleeping rough, and two had been temporarily sleeping in caravans.

The majority of the clients had had some experience of private renting before moving into their current tenancy. Thirteen had not rented before, or within the last ten years. Most of these had been in social housing tenancies or in a series of temporary housing situations. Only ten of the clients interviewed were moving directly from one private tenancy to another. Schemes had helped twenty-nine of the clients secure accommodation in self-contained flats or houses, and 10 had been helped into shared houses, bedsits, lodgings or bed and breakfast hotels. The majority of the clients had, at the time of the interview, been living in their accommodation for between seven and 12 months.

Clients' responses to services

Finding somewhere to live

The five case study schemes helping the clients had, between them, three approaches to helping clients find somewhere to live: the London Scheme found clients places to stay from its approved vacancy list; the Metropolitan Scheme issued a list of unvetted vacancies; and the Counties Scheme, the Westerbury Scheme and the Charity Scheme all offered a combination of supported search help and giving contacts from an approved vacancy list. Clients' responses to each of these approaches will be discussed in turn.

The London Scheme was the most formalised approach, and the one least appreciated by the clients. The clients, living in temporary accommodation, had been approached by the scheme with an offer of longer-term housing in the private sector. The scheme discussed with the clients what sort of housing they needed, and then made them a single offer of a property which they considered met their requirements. Clients were often given only one choice of property, and almost all were unhappy with this. Many complained that the property they felt obliged to move into was not appropriate to their household's needs - usually because there was an insufficient number of bedrooms.

In direct contrast, the Metropolitan List offered a minimum of help in finding somewhere to stay, in issuing a weekly updated list of unvetted vacancies. One of the clients appreciated the fact that the scheme allowed them free use of the telephone, but in general terms clients were not happy with the list. The list simply reproduced landlord contacts from the paper, which meant that many of the vacancies advertised were for properties where the landlord was unwilling to let to people on housing benefit. Clients had as a consequence wasted time and money making fruitless enquiries. For example, one client with a disability had looked at 12 places on the list, which had all been unsuitable or did not take people on benefits.

Despite the differences between these two schemes in the help with finding somewhere to stay, the clients of both had the expectation that standards of vacancies they were given access to would be high. For example, one of the London Scheme clients commented of the scheme, *'Well, they're good, they get you a good property. If it's not up to their standard it won't be on their register'*. Clients of the London Scheme who were not happy with the condition of their property blamed the council for not vetting more closely. Similarly, clients using the Metropolitan Scheme considered that if the scheme was issuing a list, then it was reasonable to expect that the properties on the list would be of a fair standard. One client had looked at three properties on the list and

> *last one we looked at, it were just down the road from here, and it really stunk you know, I mean why they'd got it on the housing list I don't know...I think that* [they] *should inspect them first to tell whether they're actually fit for living in.*
>
> (Client, Metropolitan Scheme)

Clients' response to the other three schemes was less critical. Although each of these schemes offered help in looking and kept an approved vacancy list, assistance had evidently been tailored to each client's particular needs. Some clients had been given a 'DSS-friendly' list and had been happy with that: *'you've got to make some sort of effort yourself'*. Other clients said that schemes had gone through the newspapers with them, driven them to see properties, and called them up when they had heard about vacancies. The only disadvantage which was expressed about this way of helping was that some clients looking for themselves would have liked more guidance on deciding which places would be suitable.

From the point of view of the client, therefore, assistance with finding somewhere to stay should include either directly vetting properties, or helping clients to define what standards were acceptable. This point was underlined by clients' responses to questions about how they themselves assessed property conditions. For the most part, clients considered the merit of a property on the strength of whether it was clean, dry, tidy, and in reasonable repair. Few of the clients thought about such issues as gas or fire safety: when asked if they considered these things, one of the clients replied, *'I don't, I mean, who does?'*, and another, *'I didn't really have any thought about it to be honest. I has never really crossed my mind. It should do really'*.

Setting up the tenancy

Clients were asked about help with setting up the tenancy. All the schemes, with the exception of the Metropolitan Scheme, gave help by negotiating rent; all offered to check tenancy agreements; and the two schemes giving deposit guarantees made out furniture inventories. Clients responses to help with these things were mixed: some services were considered valuable, whilst others were seen as unnecessary or irrelevant.

For example, most of the clients seemed fairly confident about the idea of negotiating the rent themselves. The majority of the clients who had let before, for example, had in their previous tenancy thought about negotiating their rent with the landlord. They had not done so, however, because they considered the rent to be reasonable. Three clients had actually tried negotiation and had failed, but four had tried and been successful. Only one client said they felt that they would not negotiate, because they might lose their tenancy.

On being asked whether the schemes had been involved in negotiating the rent, only the London Scheme clients considered that the scheme had in some way influenced the rent level. This feeling was largely expressed through clients commenting that they could do nothing about the rent because it was all decided between the scheme and the landlord. One of the clients thought that the rent he was paying was far too high and, given a choice, he would have tried to negotiate it down or move to somewhere cheaper. Clients of the other schemes were uncertain about any possible influence the scheme may have had over the rent. It may have been the case that the schemes had been directing clients to landlords who were already charging reasonable rents. Certainly the majority of clients said that negotiation on their current properties had been unnecessary, since the rents charged by the landlords were thought to be low or reasonable.

Clients were more sure about schemes' involvements with the tenancy agreement. Twenty of the clients said that the scheme had looked at the tenancy agreement, and explained it to them. Five of the clients said that the scheme had not been involved, and they would have liked them to have been. Although some of the clients were quite confident about dealing with tenancy agreements themselves, others found the agreement difficult to understand: *'it's all in a different language really'*. It was thought to be useful having access to someone willing to check the document:

> *...if you don't know what you're doing you can sign anything and you don't know what you're signing and that's it. I mean, like you could sign something where he says, 'Oh, I can enter your property at any time day or night', and you've signed it and you won't know because some landlords can do that.*
>
> (Client, Metropolitan Scheme)

A small number of clients appeared quite unconcerned about whether or not they understood the agreement. One of the clients was asked whether the scheme had explained the tenancy, and replied that she could not remember, *'but it doesn't really bother me'*.

Only two schemes helped by completing any sort of furniture or condition inventory, although these were only completed for furnished tenancies. None of the clients had anything to say about the virtue or otherwise of the completion of inventories. The clients evidently did not consider this process to be particularly beneficial to them, and were indifferent as to whether schemes completed them or not.

To summarise, from the point of view of clients some sorts of help with finding and setting up a tenancy were considered more valuable than others. Although schemes often thought that their clients did not attempt to negotiate on rents because they perhaps did not feel confident or secure enough to do so, clients themselves said that they often did not try because the rent charged seemed to be reasonable. It should be stressed, however, that there were some clients who did feel unable to negotiate: *'I just had to accept the rent and that's it, otherwise we'd be on the street'*. Schemes' help in this area might best be concentrated on making sure that clients get access to vacancies where reasonable rents were charged. Help with understanding tenancy agreements was usually valued. By contrast, the practice of completing furniture inventories was seen by clients as something irrelevant to them. It may be that schemes could work to educate clients on the usefulness of inventories as a means of avoiding disputes with landlords at the end of tenancies.

Help with deposits

Four of the schemes gave some sort of help with the requirement to pay a deposit, although the help varied. Two of the schemes gave deposit guarantees, and two negotiated with the landlord for a reduction in the deposit asked for. Because of the variety of experiences, each of the schemes will be discussed in turn. The London Scheme required landlords using the scheme not to ask clients for a deposit. Some, but not all, of the clients were aware that the council had dealt with this requirement on their behalf. Most of these clients had had limited experience of private renting, and did not know that a deposit might be payable. The Metropolitan Scheme also helped with deposits by negotiation, but this tended to be more immediately understood by the clients to have taken place on their behalf. One of the clients had been asked for £180 from the landlord, and he went back to the scheme:

> *I told* [the scheme] *this, I just can't afford to get the bond and the DSS won't give it you. So they negotiated with him and he said 'Oh well, that's alright'.*
>
> (Client, Metropolitan Scheme)

Two of the schemes helped by giving either cash or guarantees to the landlord. All the clients interviewed from the Westerbury Scheme and the Charity Scheme were asked for deposits, ranging from £100 to £300. Only one of the clients could afford to pay this sum themselves, through getting a cash loan from their parents. The remaining clients were given a guarantee, a loan, or a grant. In some cases, the client was required to repay the money or to save for a deposit themselves, but this was not always the case: schemes had evidently tailored the sort of help they gave according to the client's particular situation. All the clients were very happy with the sort of help they had been given. Even the clients having to make some sort of repayment were satisfied with the help they had been given.

Only one of the schemes gave no direct help with deposits. The County Scheme referred some clients to a local charity. One of the clients who was interviewed had received from the charity a part gift/part cash loan to pay the £200 her landlord had asked for. However, most of the County Scheme clients were being helped by being directed towards landlords who were flexible about deposits. Four of the clients had been asked for deposits, but these were relatively low at between £50 and £100. In all cases the landlords had been open to negotiation about payments, and had reduced the sum initially asked for, or agreed to accept the deposit in instalments. Clients said that in these circumstances they had been able to pay the deposit asked for, although one of the clients - paying off a £100 deposit at £1 a week - said that he would have preferred the scheme to have given a guarantee. He was the only client aware of other types of help with deposits that might be available.

All the clients needing help to pay deposits had been assisted by schemes in one way or another, but it is difficult to draw any conclusions about the sort of help with deposits which was generally preferable, since clients did not have the experience to compare different sorts of help. Almost all were happy with the help that they had been given, even if the assistance might have incurred some cost to the client, such as negotiating the cost down but not away, or requiring the client to save.

Help with rent in advance

None of the schemes gave help with rent in advance by making a single payment of advance rent to the landlord but four gave other kinds of help, including negotiation with the landlord, encouragement to the client to make a social fund claim, and making rent payments. Similarly to its help with deposits, the London Scheme required landlords not to ask clients for rent in advance payments. Again, none of the clients were aware that this sort of arrangement had been made. Their views tended to echo the comment made by one client: *'the* [scheme] *dealt with that side'*. Again, as with the deposits, the clients showed no appreciation of this help: it had evidently been expected.

The County Scheme also helped in a similar way, by directing clients to landlords unlikely to ask for large sums of money. Although almost all the landlords still asked for some cash up front, the amount of money asked for was often small: one client, for example, was only asked for £10, being two weeks' estimated shortfall on the housing benefit payment. The clients were generally not aware that help may have been given to them by getting them in contact with this sort of landlord. When asked if they had wanted help with rent in advance, they said that none was necessary, since they could afford the amount the landlord wanted.

There were two schemes which did not give help with rent in advance beyond encouragement to make a social fund claim. In the case of the Metropolitan Scheme, it was quite common for clients to get payment through the social fund for rent in advance, but none of the clients interviewed had had any help with an application. One of the clients had made a social fund claim, but it took some time to come through: '*I had to keep going up to me landlord, in person, and telling him that I still wanted* [the] *place and I were in a bit of trouble with me rent*'. She concluded that the situation would have been less stressful if the scheme had helped by giving some assurances to the landlord. Two of the clients of the Westerbury Scheme had been encouraged to make social fund claims and both had been successful, although neither client gave any clear indication of the scheme's role in securing the claim.

A clear assessment by clients of help with rent in advance was therefore hindered by the possibility that they may have been unaware of the help given. The clients who were aware of the help - the Charity Scheme clients - were happy with the system of rent payment. Clients of the other schemes perhaps did not appreciate that schemes were directing them towards landlords more open to negotiation on rent in advance. Looking at another type of rent in advance help, there was some dissatisfaction with the idea of applying for social fund payments for rent in advance. The time taken for the application to be processed meant that clients were in danger of having the landlord let the property to someone else.

Help with housing benefit

All the schemes offered their clients housing benefit help which went beyond making the initial application, and often included help with appeals. Most of the clients appreciated advice given about the housing benefit application form, which was considered to be over-long and confusing:

> *The advice was the best thing about it. I used to ring the DSS up and they didn't know and said 'Sorry, we can't help you', and ring the council up and I used to spend pounds on the phone - money that I didn't*

have - using the phone and everything else. And then they sent me to [the scheme] *and I came here and I was really impressed with them. He told me what form I'd need to get and everything else.*

(Client, Charity Scheme)

In almost all cases, the client was happy to have the housing benefit made over directly to the landlord, to take away a source of temptation and to dispense with the problem of having to pay the rent personally. Only one client said that he preferred to have the rent paid directly to him, and this was because he thought that he could then withhold rent if the landlord was slow in completing repairs.

Because the housing benefit cheque went directly to the landlord, tenants were generally unclear about how long it took to be processed. Clients were, however, pleased that the scheme was available to find out what had happened to claims, and hurry them along:

Rather than me going up and badgering some little office clerk, they can ring up the head honcho and say 'Oy, what's going on here?'. That's fairly useful - it does cut down the time.

(Client, Charity Scheme)

There was also agreement on the value of schemes in dealing with shortfalls. The London Scheme operated in such a way that shortfalls would not arise. Twenty-one of the remaining clients did have a shortfall, and in around half these cases the scheme had appealed or was in the process of appealing to the housing benefit office for a revision of the benefit payment. In many cases, the shortfall had either been removed or was reduced considerable. Clients evidently relished having someone both knowledgeable and willing to advocate their cause:

That was a great help because he's a really good speaker. He's got all his files and everything and he was just able to throw things at them.

(Client, Charity Scheme)

In summary, the majority of the clients appreciated any help with housing benefit they could get, including help with the application and with chasing up the claim once it had been submitted. The clients were particularly appreciative of help given with appeals against housing benefit levels which incurred large shortfalls.

Tenancy support

From the point of view of clients, there were three aspects of tenancy support which evoked some comment: help given with moving in; visits to make sure that the client had settled in alright; and going back to the scheme if there were any difficulties with landlords. Not all the schemes offered help with all these things: it was the intention of the London Scheme, for example, to set up the tenancy as an independent relationship between landlord and tenant, and to have no further dealings. The other schemes offered help which was more protracted.

A third of the clients said that they would have liked some help in moving possessions. In some cases, this help was given by the scheme, and clients were very grateful. A group most especially in need of help was the families being assisted by the London Scheme, since they usually had a large amount of possessions which required the use of a van to move. One of the families had found this situation particularly difficult, and said that even just being given the loan of a van from the council would have been a great help. One of the clients not getting any help said that in the end she had had to get a loan from the social fund to pay for the hire of a van:

> *...when you get these loans off the social...you've got to try and pay that back which leaves you short for the next six months or whatever it is, of a fiver or a tenner a week they're taking off.*
>
> (Client, Charity Scheme)

As well as help moving possessions, some clients moving into unfurnished property said that they would like help with acquiring furniture and kitchen equipment. For some, the attraction of living in the private rented sector was the fact that furnished tenancies were available, otherwise they would be moving into empty properties:

> *Well when you've got a private house you've got a washing machine and a cooker and stuff and everything's furnished, so all you have to do is put your own bits and pieces in. If you get a council house there's nothing in it.*
>
> (Client, London Scheme)

Some of the clients going into unfurnished tenancies said that the scheme had helped them in giving them information about agencies which could help with furniture and kitchen equipment. One client said that the scheme's parent organisation, which ran a furniture warehouse, had fully furnished his unfurnished flat, including giving a fridge and a cooker.

Three of the schemes continued to visit the clients, to make sure that they had settled in alright. There was a mixed reaction to the idea of this sort of visit, often dependent on the client's degree of experience with private renting. The London Scheme did not visit the tenant immediately, but checked later on to see that the tenancy was continuing as a means of ensuring that the landlord was not defrauding the council. Clients with the scheme who had not rented before tended to be critical of this policy:

> *I think the thing I've noticed is that they make sure that they meet their legal obligations. Like, they offer you a house and that's it, wash their hands...And you have to deal with everything else.*
> (Client, London Scheme)

> *A lady did visit after about three months, so it was not immediate. I would prefer a person from* [the scheme], *when they give accommodation to a person, two or three weeks later to just go and see if they're coping alright. Just a bit quicker, three months is a bit...by that time it's too late.*
> (Client, London Scheme)

Clients of the other schemes tended to have more experience of private renting, and for these people, a 'settling-in visit' was considered to be 'nice', but extended visits were thought to be unnecessary, and in some cases either irritating or an invasion of privacy. When asked about whether they wanted this sort of visit, clients' responses were often wry: *'I'm old enough to look after myself I think'* or *'It's like having Big Brother isn't it?'*. The lack of interest in this kind of support was evidently a reflection of schemes targeting their assistance at people capable of living independently.

Although the idea of having extended visits was not entirely welcomed by the clients, sorting out budgeting was one area in which clients might have appreciated more help. Seventeen of the clients said that they had had difficulty budgeting, and were struggling to keep up with bills. However, only two of the clients had had help with their finances from the scheme. Although the difficulties clients were having was often a reflection of the low incomes they were living on, schemes could give help by advising on budget accounts with gas and electricity boards, making sure that clients were receiving all the benefits they were entitled to, and give advice on debt management.

A further aspect of tenancy support was help given in liaising with the landlord when repairs were necessary. All the schemes offered this sort of help to their clients. In the majority of cases, the clients said that if anything came up, they would go to the scheme for help, although many thought that it not would often be the case that circumstances would warrant that sort of action, and they felt confident enough to deal with any eventuality. Some instances were given where the scheme had successfully persuaded the landlord to complete a repair, but in a couple of cases the scheme's intervention had not resulted in any improvement.

Looking at tenancy support in general terms, therefore, shows that clients appreciated help given at the start of the tenancy, particularly with moving their possessions, and sorting out budgeting. Indeed, clients not receiving this help said that they would find it useful. Extended visits following this initial period were not enthusiastically welcomed. Although many of the clients were offered help by the scheme if problems arose with the landlord, some of the clients said that they could not foresee any circumstances where the scheme's intervention would be necessary, and they in any case felt able to deal with situations which might arise.

Clients' evaluation of schemes

The clients were asked a series of questions to gain an impression of their overall evaluation of the schemes, including what they considered to be the good and bad things about the scheme generally, whether they would have managed to secure a tenancy without the help of the scheme, and what would be the most important help which could be given to someone trying to secure accommodation. The feature most often mentioned by clients as being a good thing about the scheme was the fact that it was willing to listen to and support the client during an obviously stressful time. Schemes *take the weight off your shoulders*. According to two clients, talking about the Charity Scheme and the County Scheme respectively, good things about the scheme included:

> *The door's always open, which is helpful, you know, because when you're unemployed all you get is shut doors all the time.*
>
> (Client, Charity Scheme)

> *Some kind of caring attitude, I suppose, as much as anything, being treated as though* [you] *are important and not just 'Oh, he's a second-class citizen looking for somewhere to live. We'll give him a hole in the ground somewhere.*
>
> (Client, County Scheme)

The next most commonly cited good feature of schemes was the help given with deposits or rent in advance:

> *...for people who want to go into private renting...if they basically haven't got the money to pay for the deposit and the rent in advance, then they haven't got a cat in hell's chance. No way.*
>
> (Client, Charity Scheme)

Other good things included the fact that the scheme dealt with the client quickly, that it was available to help when trouble arose with the landlord, and that it helped to find suitable, good quality properties.

Few of the clients said that the scheme they were helped by had any bad features, although there was one exception. Most of the clients of the Metropolitan List considered that the scheme's list was directing them towards poor quality accommodation, and so offered little assistance in the process of finding somewhere to stay.

When asked to evaluate the importance of the scheme in helping them to secure accommodation, around half of the clients (19) said that they would not have been able to secure their present accommodation without scheme help. This was particularly the case with the clients using the Charity Scheme and those using the Westerbury Scheme, both of which gave assistance with advance payments, and almost all of whose clients said that the schemes help had been invaluable. None of the clients of the Metropolitan Scheme said that they would have been unable to find accommodation without the scheme's help.

To summarise, clients' own evaluation of schemes showed that the aspects of schemes most appreciated was not a definable service, but the schemes' being a source of support during the process of securing new accommodation. The access service by far most frequently cited as being a good feature of the scheme, and also considered to be the most crucial help which could be given to someone, was help with advance payments and in particular assistance with deposits. Most of the clients who said that the scheme had been crucial to their being able to secure accommodation were being helped by schemes offering assistance with advance payments. Help given in finding somewhere to stay was considered relatively unimportant, which indicates that assistance with advance payments in itself widens the choice of available accommodation.

Clients' willingness to stay in scheme tenancies

A final aspect of the evaluation of schemes from the clients' perspective is analysis of whether clients themselves were willing to stay in the tenancies which had been created. In all, 27 of the clients said that they were satisfied with their accommodation, most of whom had renewed or rolled over their tenancy agreement at least once. Twelve were dissatisfied, however, and their dissatisfaction largely revolved around the fact that the properties were in poor condition or the rents were too expensive. Four of the five Metropolitan Scheme clients who were interviewed said that they were unhappy with conditions in the tenancies secured from the schemes' unvetted vacancy list, and were moving out for that reason.

All 12 of the dissatisfied clients were intending to move out, as were a further 16 of the clients who said that they were satisfied with their tenancies. Most of these clients said that they intended to move out once a tenancy became available in either a council or housing association property, and all these clients were on the council's waiting list. Four of the clients said that they would move out soon to pursue further or higher education courses, or to look for work in another area. Two of the clients had been asked to leave by their landlord, who wanted to sell the property.

Although some of the clients were happy with their property, and intended to stay for as long as possible, the majority evidently considered that the schemes' helping them into private sector tenancies constituted a short-to-medium-term solution to their housing need. Fifteen of the clients said that given a free choice, they would prefer to rent from the council or a housing association, and ten said that they wanted to move into owner occupation once they got work. Only eight of the tenants said that private renting was their tenure preference.

Conclusion

This chapter has looked at access help from the point of view of clients and has focused on responses to individual scheme services, clients' overall evaluation of schemes, and clients' willingness to continue living in the tenancies set up by the scheme. There was an ambiguous response to the range of services offered, with some clients feeling more confident about dealing with some aspects of securing accommodation than others. Services thought to be particularly valuable were the vetting of properties, explaining tenancy agreements, help with advance payments, and assistance with housing benefit. Few clients welcomed extended tenancy support, but the need for help with moving in - particularly with respect to help moving possessions - was frequently reported. Difficulties clients were having with sorting out bills indicated that clients should, early on in the tenancy, be made aware of possible sources of help with budgeting.

Clients' own evaluation of the good and bad points of the schemes they were helped by showed that the most valued aspect of the help was not any specified service, but schemes' willingness to listen to the client, and being available to offer advice and support throughout the process of moving from their current housing situation into the new tenancy. Most of the clients receiving help with advance payments said that they would not have been able to secure their tenancy without it.

Most of the clients said that they were happy with the tenancies that had been secured, and some said that they intended to stay for as long as possible. The majority of the tenants, however, wanted to move - some because property conditions were not good, and others because they preferred to rent from the council or a housing association, or hoped to own their own place once they started work.

Chapter Ten
Landlords

Introduction

Much of this report has looked at the issue of access from the point of view of project managers and clients. This chapter offers an evaluation of help with access from the point of view of landlords. None of the schemes set out with the primary intention of helping landlords, although most acknowledged that it was necessary to keep landlords happy to ensure a continued supply of vacancies for their clients. The chapter will ask whether landlords were satisfied with schemes' involvement with: finding tenants; setting up tenancies; deposits; rent in advance; housing benefit; and tenancy support, including dealing with the end of tenancies. Assessment will then be made of landlords' judgements of schemes' good and bad points, and whether landlords would be willing to pay for scheme services. The chapter begins by characterising the landlords, and outlining the differences between the types of landlords dealt with by each of the case schemes.

Landlord characteristics

Most of the landlords (29) were what has been termed 'sideline' landlords, and let to supplement their main income. The majority of the properties had been bought for the purpose of acquiring rental income from lettings. Between them, the landlords had a total of 519 lets, 53 per cent of which were furnished and 74 per cent of which were in self-contained accommodation. Appendix two comprises tables which give a detailed breakdown of landlord characteristics.

The five case study schemes had each tapped into a specific niche within the rental market. The landlords taking clients from the London scheme tended to be sideline landlords who had only one furnished self-contained property, which they had been letting for less than five years. The Charity Scheme landlords included three managing agents, and was a group which clearly had a greater experience of letting: most had been letting for over six years, and the majority had more than seven lettings. The Westerbury Scheme landlords fell between these two extremes. Although most of the landlords had been letting for less than five years, they tended to have a higher number of lettings than the London Scheme landlords. The Metropolitan Scheme landlords were similar to the Westerbury landlords, but included three landlords each having more than 10 lets in shared housing. By contrast, the County Scheme landlords almost all offered a number of lets in shared accommodation, some of which included rooms in bed and breakfast hotels.

Altogether, the landlords were letting to a total of 94 tenants from access schemes. Seven of the landlords were not letting to scheme tenants at the time of the interview, but had done so in the recent past. The number of scheme tenants to whom the landlord had let varied. The Westerbury, Charity and London Scheme landlords had each taken less than ten scheme tenants. Seven of the Metropolitan and County Scheme landlords had taken more than 11, and two of these landlords had had more than twenty. Similarly, experience of letting to tenants in receipt of housing benefit varied across the group of landlords. The Metropolitan and County Scheme landlords were already likely to have a large proportion of housing benefit tenants, whereas landlords using the other schemes were unlikely to have had extensive experience of letting to people on benefit.

Landlords' experience of scheme services

Finding tenants

In the case of three of the landlord groups (the London, Metropolitan and County Scheme landlords) the majority of the landlords first came into contact with the scheme because they thought that the scheme would give them access to people wanting to rent. These three schemes ran either an approved or an unvetted vacancy list. Landlords of the other two schemes generally first heard about them through prospective tenants who said that the scheme would help them with advance payments.

All the landlords were asked how they chose their tenants. In looking to fill their vacancies, the landlords tended not to be too prescriptive about the sort of tenant they wanted. The majority of landlords said that they trusted to their experience and instinct, and made a decision about whether to take a particular tenant after meeting and talking with them. By far the strongest response on the type of tenants they would and would not prefer was the desire not to let to people with some sort of specified problem: people who were on drugs, people who had been convicted of sex offences, people who were alcoholics and people with criminal records. Some landlords had preferences with respect to household type, age and gender, but these were largely a consequence of having to fill a particular vacancy where not all tenants would be appropriate. For example, one landlord only wanted tenants in their early 20s, since he was letting rooms in shared houses where the other tenants were around that age. Only a minority of landlords expressed a preference according to economic status.

Thus, the landlords in the sample could be fairly flexible about the tenants they let to, so long as the tenant appeared to be appropriate for the particular vacancy. Landlords were asked about their experience of having the scheme find them possible tenants: not all the landlords considered that their experience had been a good one. All the landlords' responses to this question were classified, as either favourable or unfavourable. The number of comments under each classification was roughly equal, with a smaller number of landlords being more neutral in their judgement. Around 14 responses were favourable, noting that appropriate clients had been sent, that the scheme had saved them the time, money and hassle, and that it was good that the scheme could also provide information on the tenant. In all these respects, the scheme was viewed as preferable to advertising or using a letting agent.

There were 13 unfavourable responses, however. The majority of these centred around the fact that the tenants had not been suitable. In one case, for example, a man convicted of sexual offences was sent to landlord running a bed and breakfast hotel filled mostly with young single mothers. Other landlords reported that clients had caused trouble or damage. These difficulties were, according to the landlords, a consequence of the scheme not vetting clients closely enough. One landlord, in talking about clients from the scheme, commented:

> *...they'll go in there and give them any old story and because they're a charity they listen to the story and accept what these people say to them. And of course when they come up and move in it's a different case you know.*
>
> (Landlord, County Scheme)

Vetting was thought to be especially important by the landlords who had not let to this sort of client group before, and who tended to make distinctions between the 'deserving' and 'undeserving' homeless:

> *...a lot of the homeless are homeless through their own fault, because they are troublemakers for one reason or another, and* [the scheme] *have got to get their act together and weed these people out, because if they don't weed them out, the people in the private sector are not going to let to them...some people will never treat anything right, never be responsible.*
>
> (Landlord, Charity Scheme)

Thus, landlords using the schemes to find tenants had mixed experiences. Landlords who had not used a scheme to find tenants generally did not think that using this service would carry any advantages. In particular, the Charity Scheme landlords considered that their taking on scheme tenants was a charitable act, helping people in housing need who otherwise would not be taken on. These landlords said that they could find tenants quite easily, and could not foresee a situation in which they would actively seek tenants from the scheme.

In summary, therefore, it was landlords at the lower end of the sector who had more appreciation of schemes helping them find tenants, probably because their turnover of tenants was much quicker than landlords offering self-contained accommodation. For all landlords, a scheme's usefulness rested on whether clients were vetted before being passed on to the landlord, and on efforts made by the scheme to ensure that the client was actually suitable for the landlord's vacancy.

Setting up a tenancy

Not all the schemes were closely involved with setting up tenancies. Neither the County Scheme nor the Metropolitan Scheme were actively involved, although either would help if the client or landlord requested it. Landlords were questioned about scheme involvement in rent negotiation, signing the tenancy agreement, and completing furniture inventories. Although they were not unhappy with the services schemes offered which helped setting up tenancies, the landlords were often indifferent to whether or not this sort of service was provided.

Landlords' response to rent negotiation varied. All the landlords involved with the London Scheme had been compelled to negotiate, as a requirement of being involved in the scheme. Most had had to accept a rent that was below the market rate. Although some of the landlords considered that this reduction was offset by not having to pay letting or managing agent fees, others were more resentful. Only two of the landlords of the other schemes recalled that the scheme had had an impact on the rent level: one landlord was advised on the rent to charge by the Metropolitan Scheme; and another landlord was persuaded by the Westerbury Scheme to include the water rates in with the rent, so that the client would not have to pay the charge separately. Of the remaining landlords, many had said that the scheme had considered the rent charged to be reasonable, and so negotiation was unnecessary.

Most of the landlords, however, had not been approached from the scheme at all with respect to negotiation on the rent. The landlords themselves indicated, however, that they were open to negotiation. Sixteen landlords said that they had in the past let a property at less than the rent originally charged. Most had done so because they thought that, although the tenant could not afford the full rent, they would look after the property and might stay for a while. For example, when asked under what circumstances he would reduce the rent, one landlord replied:

> *Under the circumstances that a person seemed to be right or seemed to be stuck and just for the sake of £5 or £10 a week you're better off with someone in the long term than someone in for two months wrecking the place.*
>
> (Landlord, Metropolitan Scheme)

Although in some cases this negotiation had taken place at time of the tenants' first approach to the landlord, in other cases the negotiation had happened once the level of the housing benefit shortfall became clear: 14 of the landlords who had experience of shortfall said that they either waived the cost, or required the tenant to pay only part of the top-up. Again, none of the landlords said that schemes had been involved in negotiating the shortfall payment.

Schemes were more proactive in looking over tenancy agreements. Both the deposit guarantee schemes were always involved in providing or checking the agreement, although the other schemes were only sometimes involved. The Metropolitan Scheme provided agreements, and three of the landlords who had been interviewed took advantage of this service. Almost all the landlords provided tenancy agreements themselves, and most of those that did not do so offered a licence agreement. Most of the landlords considered it to be their responsibility to explain the agreement to the client, and the client's responsibility to make sure that they understood. Some landlords thought that scheme involvement was not entirely necessary:

> *...it's for the landlord and the tenant to agree between them. Then if it doesn't suit either party, either party hasn't got to accept it have they?*
>
> (Landlord, County Scheme)

Other landlords were slightly more appreciative, especially when they had minimal experience of letting. One landlord considered that the London Scheme involvement with the legal aspect of the tenancy was *'quite a relief actually'*, and was pleased that responsibility had been taken by the scheme. In general terms, however, landlords tended to be indifferent to scheme involvement with the tenancy agreement, although none had any objection to the scheme checking the document.

Interest amongst landlords for the idea of completing furniture inventories varied. Around half the landlords did not complete an inventory, and usually gave the reason that the properties were let unfurnished. Even the landlords letting furnished properties often dismissed completing inventories as being too time-consuming (*'I've got better things to do'*) or unnecessary since they said they could remember what was in each room. Some said that they accepted pilfering as inevitable. Three of the schemes completed furniture inventories or checked the inventories made out by the landlord, although most of the landlords in these cases did not consider this activity to be beneficial to them. There was only one case in which the landlord considered that the inventory had been particularly advantageous, since it had eased the process of settling the bond at the end of the tenancy. Another landlord said that they would have like to have the scheme involved, since it would have saved him having to do it himself.

To summarise, schemes' giving help in setting up tenancies was not always viewed with enthusiasm by landlords, who often did not consider such involvement to be necessary. Schemes' involvement with tenancy agreements and furniture inventories was not often thought to be essential or beneficial. Few of the schemes had attempted to negotiate on rents, but landlords' reporting their willingness to reduce rents in certain circumstances indicates that more schemes should try this approach.

Deposits

Only two of the schemes gave guarantee help with deposits: the Charity Scheme and the Westerbury scheme, the latter sometimes giving cash if the landlord would not accept a guarantee. The other three schemes usually helped by negotiation. The London Scheme required landlords not to ask for a deposit. Some of the landlords were unhappy with this situation, and felt themselves to be in a vulnerable position should the client choose to damage the property. Two of the landlords simply assumed - wrongly - that the council had given some sort of verbal guarantee of good behaviour and would recompense the landlord if any damage occurred. For one landlord, the fact that the rent was 'guaranteed' because it came through the housing benefit system was enough recompense for not getting a deposit payment.

Looking at the remaining deposit-negotiating schemes, only two of the landlords recalled being approached by the scheme to negotiate the deposit on behalf of a particular client. Similarly to the findings collected on rent negotiation, many of the landlords who had not been asked by schemes to negotiate on the deposit said that they were open to that sort of approach. Many had, in the past, waived or reduced the payment or accepted it in instalments. However, these were all landlords towards the bottom end of the market, used to dealing with clients on limited incomes. For example, one bed and breakfast landlord with clients using the County scheme said *'there's no point asking tenants coming here for a deposit, they're all unemployed'*. By contrast, one of the Westerbury landlords, offering *'the sort of property you or I would want to live in'*, was more adamant about receiving payment:

> *...we won't consider tenants suitable if they can't find their deposit monies. So if a tenant appears to be suitable on every front, except they cannot find their deposit, well that's really too bad...we can't accept them - they have to have the money.*
>
> (Landlord, Westerbury Scheme)

Not all landlords, therefore, were open to negotiation on deposits. There were 14 landlords who had received written guarantees in the place of deposit payments. Four of these landlords said that they would have preferred a cash payment to have been made. In two cases this was because the landlord felt more secure with a cash payment:

> *I would prefer that the actual payment was made. I don't question the guarantee, but* [the scheme] *are a company and if they fail then our guarantee is worthless. It's not the same as having the cash in your hand and it's on deposit somewhere just in case.*
>
> (Landlord, Westerbury Scheme)

In the other two cases, the landlords objected to the type of guarantee issued: it had not covered rent in arrears, and had left each landlord out of pocket. Another landlord, although accepting a guarantee, could also foresee this as a difficulty:

> *...there's a little less security there than if you had a cash deposit, because if somebody's a Council-paid tenant and they've given a cash deposit, and there's a problem, you've got money in hand but with the* [scheme] *you haven't because you can only actually claim for damage.*
>
> (Landlord, Charity Scheme)

Another criticism was levelled at the issue of guarantees: they did not require any financial input from the client, who then lacked an incentive to keep up the tenancy. One landlord, having lost money on a client who had left owing rent, commented:

> *I think that if the tenant that has just vacated...had paid the deposit out of their own monies, they may have been a bit more responsible - because having paid the money out, it's theirs, whereas they didn't see the deposit in the first place from* [the scheme] *so it's not quite the same... The* [cash] *deposit is a very good way of doing things, because it's almost like as fidelity bond really, it is the tenant's own money and they see that as their own money, and they will do all they can to get it back at the end of the tenancy.*
>
> (Landlord, Westerbury Scheme)

This comment reflected other points made by landlords, when asked to specify how much they decided deposits should be, and what they were intended to cover. Many of the landlords said that it would be unfeasible to charge deposits which would reasonably be expected to cover any damage or theft by a tenant. One landlord, for example, had a York stone floor stolen by a tenant, and the cost of replacement was far in excess of the money given as a deposit. For some landlords, the deposit had a more symbolic meaning: it was a stake of money which would guarantee the tenant's good behaviour, rather than a fund which would compensate for damage or other eventualities. In this respect, having some system of access help which included the client making even a small financial contribution fulfilled the need for landlords to see that the client had a monetary stake in the success of the tenancy.

Despite the existence of these sorts of reservation, nine of the 14 landlords with guarantees were happy with them. Furthermore, those landlords who did not have guarantees expressed an interest: 23 of the 29 landlords without guarantees said they would take one. The landlords who said that they would not take a guarantee commented that they would prefer to take the cash, or that the system sounded overly bureaucratic. These landlords tended to be those towards the bottom end of the market who were asking for small payments, and who had a high turnover of tenants.

In general terms, therefore, landlords were happy with the general principle of receiving a deposit guarantee, but were unhappy that there were limits to the eventualities the guarantee covered. There was a discrepancy between the limited number of attempts from schemes to negotiate deposits, compared with the wider number of landlords open to negotiation, which indicated that this approach might successfully be tried more often. It was more likely to be the case, however, that only landlords at the bottom end of the market would respond favourably.

Rent in advance and housing benefit

Only one of the schemes offered cash help with rent in advance payments: the Charity Scheme gave rent payments to the landlord until the housing benefit was processed. The remaining schemes relied on negotiating with the landlord, with the London Scheme making it a requirement that landlords should not ask clients for rent in advance. Although some of the landlords had felt unhappy with not being able to ask for deposit money, none were unhappy about not being able to ask for rent in advance, primarily because they knew that a housing benefit payment would be made.

Only one of the remaining landlords recalled having the scheme try and negotiate on the rent in advance payment. As with deposit and rent negotiation, however, the landlords in general were open to this approach. Twenty-two of the landlords said that they had in the past waived the requirement to pay entirely, and a further six had reduced the amount asked for. The availability of housing benefit clearly had an influence on landlords' decisions to charge rent in advance. Eight of the landlords who normally required the tenants to pay rent in advance said that they would waive that payment if they could be sure that the housing benefit would be paid within a given time.

All the schemes gave some help with the housing benefit application, and 16 of the landlords commented on the way in which the scheme handled the application and other associated processes. The landlords showing the greatest degree of satisfaction were those using the Charity Scheme. These were also, incidentally, the landlords with the least experience of letting to people on housing benefit. The Charity Scheme had taken over the payment of the rent until the housing benefit was processed, which shielded the landlord from any difficulties with the application or delays in payment. With respect to other schemes, four of the landlords had been grateful because the scheme had speeded up the application, and a further two had been happy with the way in which the scheme had helped with application problems.

Of the 25 landlords who had no scheme help with housing benefit, 15 said that they did not consider such help necessary. These were landlords largely concentrated towards the bottom end of the market, with wider experience of letting to housing benefit claimants. Ten landlords, however, said that they would have liked help with speeding up the application, and with explaining rent restrictions and other housing benefit rules.

To evaluate their experience of taking scheme tenants on housing benefit, landlords were asked if there had been any difference between the tenants that they normally had, and scheme tenants with respect to housing benefit. Many of the landlords said that they did not have enough experience of letting to be able to judge, but of the remainder, 18 said that there had not been any perceptible difference. Eleven landlords said that housing benefit had been easier to deal with when a scheme became involved, especially when they operated as a sort of liaison between the benefit office and the landlord. According to one landlord:

> *I like that buffer between us, hence the scheme...There is somebody there who is not manipulated and as rigid as the* [housing benefit] *department is. You might just as well stand and talk to a robot as try to get some sense out of them. Whereas these guys are human beings and do understand that tenants have problems and we as landlords nonetheless still have bills to pay, and have got to make the thing work.*
> (Landlord, Charity Scheme)

Another landlord commented that it saw a difference simply because the housing benefit department *'takes more notice of somebody like that than they do of the landlord'*.

To summarise, as with deposits, landlords reported that there were few instances of schemes trying to negotiate on rent in advance, even though the landlords themselves said that they were open to this approach. Landlords said that they were willing to waive the payment because they knew that they could expect a housing benefit cheque. Landlords unused to dealing with housing benefit claimants were much more likely to appreciate any scheme help which sidestepped landlords having to become involved with the benefit process. Landlords with more housing benefit experience, however, often saw scheme help as unnecessary.

Tenancy support

All the schemes continued to have some contact with the landlord and the clients following the start of the tenancy. This final section will discuss three aspects of tenancy support: visits to clients; landlord advice; and help given at the end of the tenancy. Just over half of the landlords said that schemes continued to visit clients after the tenancy had been set up. The remaining landlords were unsure if such visits had taken place. The response to the visits was equivocal. Thirteen landlords were indifferent to the visits: although they did not object to them taking place, they did not see them as being particularly advantageous. A further five landlords said that they did not think that visits were necessary, and that they already kept a check on the tenants themselves. By contrast, 13 landlords thought that the visits were beneficial to the tenant, in offering support and ensuring that difficulties did not develop, and being good for relations between tenant and landlord. There were six landlords who said that schemes did not visit often enough. Some of these landlords cited tenant difficulties which they thought more effective and regular scheme visits could have prevented. These six landlords had had limited experience with dealing with housing benefit claimants, and had taken clients on the assumption that the scheme would 'police' the tenancy.

Although all the schemes said that they were available to give landlords advice and support, few of the landlords who were interviewed said that they had actually been helped by a scheme in that way. Schemes were often dealing with landlords who considered themselves sufficiently experienced to deal with any difficulties. Many said that when they had first started letting, there was *'a steep learning curve'*, and they had wanted information on tenancy law, housing benefit, and dealing with tenants. For many, this sort of advice was no longer necessary. A small minority of the landlords had had advice on housing benefit from schemes, and some went back to schemes if they had difficulties with tenants. For the most part, however, landlords considered that if they wanted advice, then the scheme would not be the first agency they would approach. Rather, they would go to solicitors, citizens' advice bureaux, or other landlords. Many landlords considered that advice from schemes was a service for the clients' benefit only.

Not all the landlords had had experience of a scheme tenancy being terminated, and so were unable to comment on any help which may have been available. However, although none of the London Scheme landlords had yet come to the end of their scheme tenancy, all offered comment on the fact that the scheme had not made it clear what would happen when the tenancies did come to an end. Most of the landlords were unhappy with being so uncertain. By contrast, the Metropolitan Scheme and County Scheme landlords were offered no help with the ending of tenancies, but were quite happy with that, since they felt perfectly able to deal with these matters themselves: *'they might take advice from me'*.

A greater degree of involvement with the end of the tenancy was expected from the schemes which offered written guarantees. Eleven landlords had between them experienced the end of 17 tenancies where the scheme had given a written guarantee. Of these tenancy terminations, five had gone through without any claim being made on the guarantee. Claims had been made against a further five, with the landlord being satisfied that things had gone smoothly. For seven of the tenancies, however, the landlord had been left out of pocket because the guarantee had not covered all the cost of the damage, none of the rent arrears, and none of the cost of the often considerable clearing up thought necessary after the tenant had left. One of the landlords said that the ending of the tenancy had been dealt with so badly by the scheme that he would not take scheme tenants again.

Thus, landlords' opinions on the value of tenancy support depended very much on the type of landlord. Less experienced landlords, who were unsure about having tenants on housing benefit, were more likely to want both advice and assurances that the scheme would continue to keep in touch with their client. Landlords with more experience tended to consider tenancy support to be irrelevant to them. For some landlords, the ending of the tenancy had been soured because the eventualities covered by the guarantees had been limited, so leaving them out of pocket.

Landlords' evaluation of schemes

Landlords were asked what they considered to be the good and bad points of the schemes they were involved with. There was a variety of responses on what might be the good points of schemes, although there were two discernable trends. A quarter of the landlords said that they liked the fact that the scheme found them tenants, and so saved the hassle of advertising. Seven of these were landlords towards the bottom end of the market, and were involved with either the Metropolitan and the County Scheme. A second trend was the number of landlords who said that involvement with the scheme had ensured regular payment of rent. Most of these landlords were involved with Charity Scheme, which offered rent payments until the housing benefit came through. Other good points cited about the schemes included the fact that the scheme provided tenancy agreements, was knowledgeable and helpful, provided tenancy support, and did not charge for their services.

Landlords highlighted a number of what they considered to be bad points about schemes. Some of the criticisms were levelled at quite basic aspects of the scheme, including staff being difficult to get hold of, or the scheme not being explained properly. The most frequently-made complaints were that clients were not adequately vetted, the scheme did not visit the clients once they had moved in, and that the deposit guarantee given was inadequate.

Landlords were asked whether they would be willing to pay for the schemes' services. The response was equivocal, and depended very much on the landlord type. For example, one landlord seeing the scheme as a means of providing tenants commented:

> *Yes, I don't see why not. At least you should be prepared to pay something because if you advertise in the paper it isn't cheap.*
> (Landlord, Metropolitan Scheme)

By contrast, one of the more up-market landlords involved with the Charity Scheme was adamant that payments would not be appropriate:

> *...at the end of the day we're giving people...that wouldn't normally be able to get into private rented accommodation, the chance to get into it. So really we're helping them.*
> (Landlord, Charity Scheme)

When asked in more general terms if there were services for which they would pay, seven landlords said that they would pay for help with housing benefit, eight would pay for a supply of tenants, and seven landlords would pay for general management support, by which most usually meant some sort of private sector leasing arrangement.

Conclusion

This chapter has discussed landlords' evaluation of their dealings with access schemes, and has highlighted the differences in attitude between landlord types. Landlords towards the bottom end of the market were more likely to value schemes for their ability to provide a regular supply of tenants. Landlords further up the market did not consider this to be an important aspect of scheme work, since they did not consider finding tenants a difficulty. For all landlords, however, schemes' ability to vet clients and provide some sort of information about them was considered valuable. Looking at other aspects of scheme involvement with landlords, it is clear that landlords with limited experience were more likely to appreciate scheme input with such matters as dealing with the tenancy agreement or sorting out housing benefit.

Few of the landlords said that the scheme had tried to negotiate with them on any of the financial aspects of securing a tenancy - deciding the rent, the deposit, or rent in advance. Most of the landlords said that, in the past, they had agreed to a lower rent or waived or reduced deposits or rent in advance, which indicates that schemes might consider this approach more frequently. Landlords welcomed the idea of deposit guarantees, although there were some reservations, which included the limited nature of the eventualities covered, and the fact that clients were not required to make a financial input themselves.

Many of the landlords were indifferent to schemes' continuing contact following the start of the tenancy, but these landlords tended to be those with more experience of taking this sort of client group on as tenants. Landlords with less experience of letting to housing benefit recipients were more likely to value schemes' continued contact with their clients.

Conclusion

Introduction

Much of this report has defined the way in which schemes deliver services which help people secure accommodation in the private rented sector. The report has highlighted different approaches to these services, in terms of discussing their advantages and disadvantages, and has also included some evaluation of schemes from the point of view of scheme managers, clients and landlords. The conclusion will begin by considering the role of access schemes as a response to housing need. In answering this question the report offers a clearer definition of the role of access help than has hitherto been available. Using that definition as its starting point, the remainder of the conclusion will then offer a series of good practice points which are hoped to be of value to organisations planning to set up, or which are running, an access scheme.

The role of access help

As Chapter one indicated, there has been a great deal of enthusiasm for the development of assistance given to people on low incomes, to help them secure access to accommodation in the private rented sector. The role of access help in dealing with housing need requires more strict definition, however. This report makes clear the fact that access help does not constitute a suitable response to street homelessness. The extensive work which has been completed on the nature of homelessness has indicated that people who have had extended experience of street homeless are more likely than other homeless groups to suffer from a range of mental and physical health problems, and so be in need of resettlement. As Chapter three and Chapter eight of this report have demonstrated, access schemes often only took on people capable of living independently without long-term resettlement support. Many schemes considered that resettlement work was a service which was outside their remit, and in any case often held the view that it was inappropriate to house clients needing resettlement in accommodation in the private sector. Landlords concurred with this view: few wanted to deal with people who had problems with addictions or disruptive behaviour.

Looking at the clients who were interviewed as part of the evaluation, only two had been street homeless at the time of their first contact with a scheme. The majority had been in a situation of sometimes acute housing need, and were clients whose tenancies might be coming to an end, or whose relatives had asked them to leave, or whose partnerships had broken down. Some of the clients were prepared to move on to yet another insecure housing situation, but others were in danger of becoming roofless unless an alternative option was presented. One scheme characterised its work with clients as prevention:

> *...averting crisis situations...but planning how they're going to move and preparing for it, rather than just ending up on somebody's floor which is a very difficult way to live and very short term.*
>
> (Manager, Westerbury Scheme)

Thus the role of access help can best be defined not as a direct solution to rooflessness, but a preventative measure enabling clients to avoid having to move through a series of insecure housing situations, risking rooflessness in the process.

Good practice

Having defined more clearly a role for help with access, the report will conclude by highlighting points of good practice. These good practice points acknowledge the diversity of help given with access: as will be made clear, not all the points given are applicable to all types of scheme, every type of client, and in each localised rental market.

Setting up and monitoring a scheme

▸ Schemes should be clear about their aims, especially with respect to the client group they intend to help and the type of landlord they hope to target. A scheme which is focused, tailoring its services to give particular assistance, is more likely to be effective than one which attempts to offer all services to all clients.

▸ Reflecting this point, funding agencies should aim to finance a greater number of more specialised access schemes, rather than fund one scheme which is intended to help all clients in all circumstances.

▸ Schemes should institute performance indicators which aim to measure degrees of satisfaction amongst clients and landlords. Monitoring the number of landlords who return to the scheme for tenants is a more telling indicator than counting the number of landlords on a register; and monitoring the number of renewed tenancies is a more useful indicator than adding up the number of tenancies which have been set up. It should be acknowledged, however, that some tenancies end for 'legitimate' reasons, with clients moving on into work or higher education or to live with partners, for example.

Funding

▶ Voluntary sector schemes should explore the possibility of joint funding arrangements with local authorities.

▶ Schemes should examine the possibility of referring agents, such as the probation service or social services departments, giving financial backing for issue of guarantees for their clients.

Referrals

▶ Schemes taking referrals should ensure that the referral agencies have a clear understanding of the criteria governing the clients helped.

▶ Schemes without a parent organisation may benefit from referral agencies vetting clients on the schemes' behalf.

Clients

▶ Schemes should anticipate that clients will not always require a full package of services, and may simply need either help with a deposit or support during the search for somewhere to stay. Schemes should try and allow the client to take some initiative.

▶ Schemes should ensure that the way in which they help clients is not so formalised that clients are 'processed' rather than listened to.

Landlords

▶ Schemes should endeavour to gain an understanding of the peculiarities of their local rental market, including rent level, standards, and advance payments usually required. Services should be tailored accordingly. For example, there is little point in offering a deposit scheme in an area where most landlords only ask for rent in advance.

▶   Schemes should aim to place some restrictions on the landlords they deal with to ensure that, at the very least, clients are not placed with landlords convicted of illegal eviction. Time spent ensuring landlords charge average, reasonable rents and have good management practices saves the scheme time in having to set up tenancies and sort out disputes.

▶   Schemes should tailor their services to appeal to different landlord types: for example, HMO/bedsit-type landlords want a reasonable supply of tenants about whom the scheme can provide some information; landlords letting self-contained accommodation often want financial incentives in the form of advance payments to take housing benefit claimants, and like the scheme to keep an eye on the tenant; reluctant landlords prefer schemes to take a more proactive role in sending appropriate clients, setting up the tenancy and dealing with the housing benefit.

Help finding somewhere to live

▶   Issuing lists of unvetted vacancies often wastes clients' time and helps to perpetuate bad tenancies and poor landlord management practices.

▶   Helping the client find somewhere to live by looking through the papers with them can sometimes be just as effective as a more formalised process of keeping an approved landlord register. Schemes should also be prepared to let clients go out and choose accommodation for themselves.

▶   Giving the client some degree of choice in the accommodation offered - even if only a choice between two properties - gives the client the opportunity to show initiative and exercise a degree of control over the help given, and so may enhance their willingness to stay in a particular place for longer.

▶   Schemes should ensure that neither the client nor the landlord believe that scheme involvement in setting up the tenancy constitutes a recommendation of the client to the landlord or vice versa.

Vetting properties

▶   Schemes should encourage their local authority to institute a register of shared property.

▶ Schemes which encourage clients to find property for themselves should consider giving the clients a tenancy and condition checklist which they can use themselves to vet accommodation, and which will enable them to make a more informed decision on whether to take a property.

▶ Schemes should aim to establish minimum standards, and strive not to use properties below these standards. Schemes giving clients access to lists of vacancies should ensure that the properties on the vacancy list meet the minimum standard.

Setting up the tenancy

▶ Schemes should ensure that both the landlord and the client are aware of their tenancy rights and responsibilities, in particular the tenant's responsibility to give notice at the end of the tenancy, and the landlord's responsibility to complete repairs.

Deposits

▶ Schemes should attempt to negotiate on deposits, particularly with landlords operating at the bottom end of the market.

▶ If no cash help is given, the scheme should still consider introducing a furniture and condition inventory to prevent the landlord unfairly retaining money which the client has paid in deposit.

▶ Schemes should monitor landlord satisfaction with guarantees, and consider expanding the guarantee if landlords are failing to return to the scheme because they are losing money as a consequence of the guarantee not covering all eventualities.

▶ Schemes should consider instituting help which includes the client having to make some payment towards the deposit - even if only £10 or £20 - or saving to cover the cost of the deposit once the guarantee is withdrawn. Encouraging the client to make a financial commitment to the tenancy enhances their willingness to make it work, and assures the landlord that the client has a monetary inducement to keep to the tenancy agreement.

Rent in advance and housing benefit

▸   Schemes should try to negotiate with landlords on rent in advance, and agree with
      the local authority some system of speeding up the housing benefit payment as
      an inducement to landlords to waive advance rent altogether.

▸   Inexperienced landlords in particular should be targeted for help with housing
      benefit.

▸   Schemes should ensure that clients are given help with applying for housing
      benefit, and are given advice in the eventuality of a large shortfall between the
      rent charged and the housing benefit payable.

Tenancy support

▸   Schemes should acknowledge that landlords with limited experience of taking
      housing benefit tenants might consider tenancy support to be a necessary scheme
      function.

▸   Schemes should be flexible about the provision of post-tenancy support, and
      anticipate that advice on budgeting may sometimes be welcome. Schemes might
      consider preparing material for circulation to clients, containing information on
      benefits and budget accounts with utility companies.

▸   Schemes should explore the possibility of offering help to clients with moving
      their possessions from one tenancy to another.

▸   Schemes should try as far as possible to achieve a neutral stance with respect to
      disputes between landlords and clients. Landlords are unlikely to come back to
      schemes which they perceive to be 'on the client's side'.

Conclusion

The report has shown that there was a wide variety of approaches taken to offering access
services, and that different approaches each carried a range of advantages and
disadvantages. Schemes often tailored their services to the peculiarities of the niche rental
market they were aiming at, and to the needs of the clients they were helping. The
findings from the case study schemes showed that most access help constituted a valuable,

and valued, response to the difficulties clients faced in attempting to secure accommodation in the private rented sector. Of particular importance, however, was the giving of financial assistance with advance payments. This sort of help meant that the search process became much easier, because clients then had access to a larger choice of properties. Schemes were also able to use advance payments as a means of securing better-quality accommodation for their clients.

References

Anderson, I., Kemp, P.A. and Quilgars, D. (1993) *Single Homeless People*, London: HMSO.

Bailey, R. (1992) 'No deposit, no return', *Inside Housing*, 21 Aug.

Bevan, M. and Rhodes, D. (1995) 'Evaluation of the capacity and the appropriateness of the private rented sector to house the homeless', unpublished draft report.

Bevan, M., Oldman, C., Rhodes, D., Rugg, J. and Third, H. (1994) 'Evaluation of the DoE s73 grant programme', unpublished report.

Bevan, M., Kemp, P.A. and Rhodes, D. (1995) *Private Landlords and Housing Benefit*, York: Centre for Housing Policy.

Carey, S. (1995) *Private Renting in England*, London: HMSO.

Department of the Environment (1989) *The Government's Review of the Homeless Legislation*, London: HMSO.

Department of the Environment (1993) *English House Condition Survey*, London: HMSO.

Department of the Environment (1995a) 'An Evaluation of the Department of the Environment's s73 programme', Housing Research Summary no.41.

Department of the Environment (1995b) 'General consent under s25 of the Local Government Act 1988 for assistance for housing accommodation leased from, or managed on behalf of, private landlords 1995'.

Green, H. and Hansbro, J. (1995) *Housing in England*, London: HMSO.

Hansard, 17 Jan 1991.

Hansard, written answers, 19 Jan 1995.

Hansard, oral answers, 13 Feb 1995.

Huby, M. and Dix, G. (1992) *Evaluating the Social Fund*, London: HMSO.

Inside Housing, 'Deposit bank urged for tenants', 2 Mar 1990.

Jenn, M. (1994) *Rent Guarantee Scheme Handbook: Housing Homeless People in the Private Rented Sector*, Manchester: Churches National Housing Coalition.

Kemp, P.A. and Rhodes, D. (1994) *The Lower End of the Private Rented Sector: A Glasgow Case Study*, Edinburgh: Scottish Homes.

Kemp, P.A., Oldman, C., Rugg, J. and Williams, T. (1994) *The Effect of Benefit on Housing Decisions*, London: HMSO.

Randall, G. and Brown, J. (1994) *Private Renting for Single Homeless People: An Evaluation of a Pilot Rent Deposit Fund*, London: HMSO.

Saunders, H. (1991) 'Pulling up the ladder', *Roof*, Sep/Oct.

Social Security Advisory Committee (1992) *The Social Fund: A New Structure*, London: HMSO.

Appendix One : Summaries of Case Study Schemes

The following pages give summaries of the case study schemes

COUNTY SCHEME

The County Scheme operated from a small south western tourist town, and covered a wide area of the largely-rural county. The parent organisation originated as a charity helping local homeless people, and at the time of the interview had a wide scale of operations which included running two hostels for the probation service, two special needs hostels and a furniture store. The approved landlord register was developed following the merging of emergency and long-term placement work.

The approved landlord register was run by two part-time workers, each working 22.5 hours. Some secretarial support was given, and fundraising was done by the parent organisation's co-ordinator. No volunteers were used. The scheme was partially funded under the s73 grant programme, which was supplemented from grants from two local district councils, the health authority and the social services.

WESTERBURY SCHEME

The Westerbury Scheme operated was operated by a housing association in a south-western town. The housing association had a Youth Project for vulnerable 16-25-year olds which comprised a hostel funded as part of a three-way service delivery agreement with the local authority and the social services department. Two large donations had been given to the Project and it was decided that these donations should be used to help hostel residents with deposits for move-on accommodation in the private rented sector. The need for help with deposits had been recognised by the Youth Project workers. It was also decided that access to the fund should be given to young people who had not been hostel residents, although the hostel residents still had priority.

There were no staff specifically employed to oversee the operation of the bond guarantee scheme, although this situation was due to change. Two of the workers employed by the Youth Project issued guarantees as part of their duties - taking perhaps half their time to do so - and were paid for this work out of the general revenue funding of the Youth Project. The Youth Project also gave the scheme use of its part-time administrator (who undertook secretarial tasks and collated the necessary evaluative data) and a special needs co-ordinator (who had responsibility for fundraising). The scheme did not use volunteers at the time of the interview, but had used single volunteers in the past to help with fundraising.

CHARITY SCHEME

The Charity Scheme, operated by a large national charity, was located in a small town in a mixed rural local authority. The scheme offered a deposit and rent payment, and took referrals from local hostels and from the probation service. Although the charity had in the past operated a day centre for the homeless in the area, at the time of the interview the charity's only function was to run the deposit and rent payment scheme.

The scheme was set up with funding from a large housing charity. A full-time co-ordinator was employed with some funding under the s73 grant programme. Two support staff were also employed for a total of 30 hours, and a book-keeping administrator worked for seven hours a week. At the time of the interview, around three or four volunteers were involved in the scheme, and were being used principally for tenant support work.

LONDON SCHEME

The London Scheme operated within the homelessness unit of an inner-city London borough, and was financed from the housing department's general funds. The scheme ran an approved landlord register, and placed families presenting as homeless or in temporary accommodation in lettings from the register. The lettings were intended to last for at least a year, after which tenants had the option of staying or of taking up the offer of council housing.

The scheme had a co-ordinator who spent approximately one third of their time on this work. The co-ordinator managed a team which included acquisition officers (inspecting new properties and agreeing rent with the landlord); lettings officers (viewing the property with the client and setting up the tenancy); and administrative officers (dealing with paperwork and housing benefit applications). The co-ordinator also checked the rent levels agreed by the acquisition officers. No volunteers were used on the scheme.

METROPOLITAN SCHEME

The Metropolitan Scheme operated in a small town which was part of a larger metropolitan local authority located in the north of England. The scheme helped people by producing an unvetted list of vacancies which was updated every week. The scheme was run by a voluntary sector organisation which ran a hostel for young teenagers, and a shop-front welfare rights centre. The parent organisation had been helping with move-on informally for some time, but it was realised that a more structure approach was necessary especially with respect to developing a closer relationship with landlords. A worker was taken on specifically to develop the vacancy list.

The worker was part-funded by s73, and part-funded from the parent organisation's own general funds. Maintaining the list and helping people secure accommodation from the list was one of the worker's tasks which also included reception duties. Follow-up work on benefit applications and difficulties with tenancies was done by an advice worker, as part of the general welfare advisory service of the organisation. Fundraising for the scheme was organised by the organisation's co-ordinator.

Interviews also took place with project managers from:

TOWNSHIRE SCHEME

The Townshire Scheme operated within the housing department of a borough council located in the east of England. The scheme offered clients cash help with deposits. Cheques were issued directly to property managers or the solicitors of landlords, and the client was required to reimburse the scheme through payments in instalments. The scheme was specifically for single non-priority homeless people on the council waiting list, although priority households have also been helped. No information was available on the background to the scheme.

The scheme was managed by a housing officer who devoted part of their time to the task, and who had some secretarial support. There was some input from the finance department which raised the cheques, and the legal department which chased clients who are in arrears with repayments. No volunteers were used.

NORTHERN SCHEME

The Northern Scheme was run as one of the services offered by a large housing charity operating in a metropolitan local authority in the north of England. Other services included day centres and resettlement projects. Money had been raised through a local charity event aimed at helping young homeless people, and the housing charity employed a project manager who earmarked the funds for use in backing deposit guarantees, specifically for single people aged 16-25. This decision had been taken after discussions with local landlords, on ways in which they could be encouraged to let to this group.

The scheme had one worker, funded under the s73 programme, who devoted half their time to this work. Support was given by the housing charity through access to secretarial assistance and a fundraiser. No volunteers were used.

CITY SCHEME

The City Scheme operated in a northern city, as part of a voluntary sector day centre and outreach project targeted at young people. The decision to set up an approved landlord register followed recognition of the increasing incidence of youth homelessness in the city.

The project worker undertook most of the tasks relating to the operation of the register and dealing with the clients. The post was part-funded under the s73 programme. The accommodation register was line-managed by the project's co-ordinator, who also dealt with fundraising. The scheme worker also had access to an administration assistant who gave secretarial support. The scheme did not use volunteers.

CHURCHES SCHEME

The Churches Scheme operated in a small south-western tourist town. One of the congregations in the town decided that it wanted to help those in housing need in the area, and a committee was set up involving members from other churches. The publication of the *Rent Guarantee Scheme Handbook* inspired the committee to give some sort of help with advance payments. At the time of the interview, the Churches Deposit Scheme gave cash help with deposits, and took clients referred from the local authority.

The scheme operated wholly from donations - mostly from churches - and *ad hoc* fundraising events. The organisers have applied for charitable status. The scheme did not have a parent organisation, and was operated wholly by volunteers, four of which gave an average of three days a month. Tasks were not devolved to particular volunteers - work was completed by whichever volunteer was available at the time.

NORTHWEST SCHEME

The Northwest Scheme operated in a north west town as part of a small voluntary sector organisation that ran a day centre, emergency nightstop accommodation and longer-stay hostel accommodation for young people. It was observed that many of the young people using the charity's services were returning after failing to settle in long-term accommodation, and so money was applied for to fund a full-time worker to help the young people secure accommodation in the private sector.

The worker took responsibility for finding young people a place to stay, and provided continuing support on an informal basis after tenancies started. Volunteers working in the hostels who befriended particular clients also continued offering support. No secretarial assistance was given, but the post was line-managed by a co-ordinator who also undertook fundraising for the organisation. The resettlement post was part-funded by the s73 programme. Remaining funds came from the organisation's general income, which included charitable trust donations and a grant from the local authority.

SOUTHWEST SCHEME

The Southwest Scheme was managed as a stand-alone project, having no parent organisation. The main purpose of the scheme was to help single non-statutory homeless people by giving deposit guarantees, but statutory homeless families were also helped as part of a service contract agreement with the local council. Initiative for the scheme followed recognition that there was limited help available to single non-statutory homeless people in the area.

The scheme had one full-time staff member, who was assisted in administrative tasks by two full-time and one part-time volunteer. The project's co-ordinator worked approximately one day a week, and had responsibility for fundraising. Funding for the project came from a range of sources including donations from local churches. The wages of the full-time worker were initially paid from a Programme Development Grant from the City Council, but this grant was limited to one year. After this year had finished, the post attracted s73 funded.

Appendix Two : Client Details

The following tables give details of the clients who were interviewed.

Key - W: Westerbury Scheme
       L: London Scheme
       C: County Scheme
       M: Metropolitan Scheme
       Ch: Charity Scheme

Table A2:1 Personal characteristics

	W	L	C	M	Ch	
Number of clients interviewed	8	7	9	5	10	39
Gender						
Male	5	3	7	1	8	24
Female	3	4	2	4	2	15
Age						
20 and under	4	0	1	1	0	6
21-25	4	1	1	1	2	9
26-40	0	3	5	2	8	18
31-65	0	3	2	1	0	6
Ethnic group						
White british	7	2	9	5	10	33
Black british	0	2	0	0	0	2
Asian	0	2	0	0	0	2
Middle eastern	0	1	0	0	0	1
Mixed	1	0	0	0	0	1

Table A2:2 Household status

Single with

no children	8	0	7	1	5	21
1 child	0	2	0	1	2	5
2 or more children	0	3	1	1	0	5
visiting child(ren)	0	0	1	0	1	2

Couple with

no children	0	0	0	0	1	1
one child	0	0	0	1	1	2
2 or more childen	0	2	0	1	0	3

Table A2:3 Economic status

	W	L	C	M	Ch	
Unemployed	3	0	4	0	0	7
Unemployed 12+ months	4	4	5	2	7	22
Disability prevents work	0	0	0	2	1	3
Part-time student	0	0	0	0	1	1
Full-time student	1	1	0	0	0	2
Full-time work	0	2	0	1	1	4

Table A2:4 Housing type

Not self-contained

Lodgings	1	0	0	0	0	1
B+B hotel	0	0	2	0	0	2
Shared house	0	0	2	0	1	3
Bedsit	1	0	1	0	2	4

Self-contained

1-bed flat	5	0	3	1	0	9
2-bed flat	1	3	0	0	1	5
1-bed house	0	0	0	0	1	1
2-bed house	0	1	1	0	5	7
3-bed house	0	3	0	2	0	5
4-bed house	0	0	0	2	0	2

On council waiting list   4   6   1   1   8   20

Appendix Three : Landlord Characteristics

The following tables give details of the landlords who were interviewed.

Key - W: Westerbury Scheme
      L: London Scheme
      C: County Scheme
      M: Metropolitan Scheme
      Ch: Charity Scheme

Table A3:1 Landlord characteristics

	W	L	C	M	Ch	Total
Number of landlords interviewed	8	6	10	9	10	43
Landlord type						
Full-time	1	0	4	4	1	10
Sideline	7	6	6	5	5	29
Managing agent	0	0	0	0	4	4
Number of years experience of letting						
Unknown	0	0	0	0	1	1
0-5	3	5	5	7	3	23
6-10	1	1	1	0	2	5
11-20	4	0	2	2	1	9
21+	2	0	0	0	3	5

Table A3:2 Landlords' lettings

Total lettings	35	18	145	76	245	519
Shared	0	0	96	28	10	134
Unshared	35	18	49	48	235	385
Furnished	12	18	141	58	5	234
Unfurnished	23	0	4	18	240	285
Scheme lettings	6	9	26	32	21	94

A - 126